BACKCOUNTRY FLIES

Tying and Fishing Florida Patterns, from Swamp to Surf

STEVE KANTNER

STACKPOLE
BOOKS
Guilford, Connecticut

Published by Stackpole Books
An imprint of The Rowman & Littlefield Publishing Group, Inc.
4501 Forbes Blvd., Ste. 200
Lanham, MD 20706
www.rowman.com

Distributed by NATIONAL BOOK NETWORK
800-462-6420

Photographs by the author unless otherwise credited

British Library Cataloguing in Publication Information available

Library of Congress Cataloging-in-Publication Data

Names: Kantner, Steve, author.
Title: Backcountry flies : tying and fishing Florida patterns, from swamp to surf / Steve Kantner.
Description: Guilford, Connecticut : Stackpole Books, [2019] | Includes index.
Identifiers: LCCN 2018040340 (print) | LCCN 2018050062 (ebook) | ISBN 9780811766203 (ebook) | ISBN 9780811737111 (paperback : alk. paper)
Subjects: LCSH: Fly fishing—Florida—Guidebooks. | Fly tying—Florida. | Florida—Guidebooks.
Classification: LCC SH483 (ebook) | LCC SH483 .K268 2019 (print) | DDC 799.12/4—dc23
LC record available at https://lccn.loc.gov/2018040340

∞™ The paper used in this publication meets the minimum requirements of American National Standard for Information Sciences—Permanence of Paper for Printed Library Materials, ANSI/NISO Z39.48-1992.

Printed in the United States of America

Contents

This osprey just caught his dinner. Predation, in one form or another, is the basis for all hook-and-line fishing. PAT FORD PHOTO

Acknowledgments

Where did all this collective knowledge come from? Some from trial and error, but also from well-known mentors and legends like Bernard "Lefty" Kreh; the late Charley Waterman; J. M. "Chico" Fernandez; the late Bob Kay, master bug-tier; the late Jack Allen, arguably the quintessential Everglades fly-rod bass guide—who, coincidentally, lived right down the street from me; and Jon Cave, whose background in guiding and casting instruction, along with his master's in Natural Resources (with special emphasis in fisheries), adds credence to whatever ditties he brings to the table.

I'd be remiss not to mention other, more recent contributors such as Dr. Martin Arostegui, who wrote the foreword to this book, and my wife, Vicki Kantner, who, along with Amy Knowles and Shelley Johnson, reread my copy and critiqued my verbiage until my ears were ringing. Also—as you can judge from the photo credits—angler/photographer Pat Ford, whose generosity and patience made this book a reality. I couldn't have done it without him. I'll admit that I'm lousy with cameras—especially big ones with fancy lenses. Pat, who isn't, brought my work up to speed with his relentless edits. Kudos also go out to Captain Mike Conner, who helped solve my salt marsh riddles, for contributing both photos and counsel, and to guide Alan Zaremba—of largemouth bass and exotics fame—for his wisdom and no-nonsense reporting.

I also wish to credit other contemporary tiers including Dr. Marcia Ely and Ron Winn of Titusville, Florida; Roan zumFelde of Naples; and Jody Moore of Fort Lauderdale—not to mention Fred Ade, aka "the Lord Mayor of Sunshine Ranches." In addition, my thanks go out to all of today's rank-and-file anglers and tiers who continue the tradition of fly-tying excellence. This is as much their work as mine. That said, my moniker appears on a pattern or two—ones I hope will prove helpful to anyone who's willing to tie and fish them. Writing this book, as I mentioned, has been a collective effort.

Learning the science helped me wrest order from chaos, both for my fishing and my tying. In order to get the lowdown, I relied on broadcast meteorologist Jennifer Gray, of CNN and HLN, to edit my gibberish—which she did zealously. Jennifer, who once lived in Miami, was a weather personality on local TV before moving to Atlanta. She's also an accomplished angler. My thanks to both Jennifer and Jonathan Finch of NOAA's Storm Prediction Center in Dodge City, Kansas, for their help on this project. (Read more about John in the "weather" sidebar on pages 3–6).

I also wish to thank editor Jay Nichols and the staff at Stackpole Books for transforming this mishmash into organized—as well as readable—content.

World-class angler and IGFA trustee Dr. Martin "Marty" Arostegui currently holds over 400 world records—nearly twice the number of his closest rival (his son, Martini). Many were caught on fly gear. Of his numerous fly records, most—to the best of his recollection—were caught on flies he tied. MARTIN AROSTEGUI PHOTO

Foreword

By Dr. Martin Arostegui

As an avid South Florida angler, I'd heard stories about Steve Kantner, the so-called Landcaptain. Once we finally met, we became friends and soon afterward, fishing buddies. It was on one of our first Everglades outings that I learned that Steve was also a master fly tier. We were fishing just off the Tamiami Trail for snook and baby tarpon.

Upon arriving at one of Steve's "hot spots," he presented me with a Muddler Minnow lookalike that he had dubbed the Rivet. Steve had designed this nondescript pattern after carefully observing the gambusia and killifish baitfish that are so abundant in backwater canal systems. Both are major forage items for both snook and tarpon that make these waters their home. Steve's Rivet imitated these baitfish to perfection, so how well we did that day was no surprise to me.

On another occasion, Steve and I were offshore in my boat, with Captain Bouncer Smith at the helm. Suddenly, a school of Bermuda chubs appeared behind our chum bag. Talk about being unprepared! We tried a number of different fly patterns without getting a sniff. But instead of yielding to frustration, we took it as a challenge, and after trial and error, we deconstructed a bonefish fly in order to make it look like the bits of ground-up fish that oozed from our chum bag. Our collaboration met with immediate success—and a pair of screaming fly reels! The best part? We solved the riddle.

Need more convincing?

South Florida has many freshwater canals that were designed to drain storm water from the state's interior in order to prevent flooding. Various invasive freshwater grasses can clog these canals and prevent the water from escaping. As a result, the authorities introduced the vegetarian Chinese grass carp to counteract this problem. While guiding clients, Steve observed that at certain times of the year, the carp congregated under fruit-bearing trees that line the canal banks. These berries are a favorite food of grass carp. Using his powers of observation and artistic creativity, Steve designed the famous Berry Fly. Made out of a cork ball the size of the berries and painted the same color, these flies behave just as a berry that fell in the water. Steve guided me to a world-record grass carp with these flies. I, in turn, have guided other anglers to world records of their own using Steve's original Kantnerberry.

I can still remember the sense of accomplishment—as well as pride—that I experienced when I caught my first fish with a fly that I not only tied but designed, all by myself. I have Steve Kantner to thank for recalling that important lesson.

Pristine Cherry Creek flows through Oakland Park, a Fort Lauderdale, Florida, suburb. This nondescript waterway serves as a nursery for snook, jacks—and, reportedly, redfish.

Introduction

Swamp to Surf, Shellcrackers to Snook

Essentially, I wrote this book for do-it-yourselfers—anglers who bust through walls of saw grass or wade off beaches and shorelines. My aim in this book is twofold: First, to provide welcome relief from that worn-out mindset that pervades less explicit volumes—the ones that fail to say "what for" and "when." Second, to provide easy-to-follow instructions on how to create (notice I didn't say "tie") the flies and fly-rod lures that unlock the secrets of those marvelous, mysterious, alternative venues that have escaped the attention of most mainstream anglers. What follows is essentially a compendium of proven designs, with some step instructions for those flies that I think require them.

I'm a longtime fancier of tannic water species—bass, snook, and tarpon—a "backwater enthusiast" who grew up fishing southeast Florida's brackish canals and ditches. Since I had no car at the time, my choices were limited, and flats skiffs, back then, were practically nonexistent. It would take years until I worked my way inland and, ultimately, to southwest Florida's mangrove salt marsh—or picked up a fly rod. Remember when Alligator Alley (then a two-lane road) was under construction? I do, and I took full advantage of the fishing it offered.

In the beginning, seeing the Glades was like visiting another, albeit foreign, planet: the birds, the miles of sunken prairies, bass for the taking—and a reliable source of hungry "trash fish." The gars and mudfish that flew under the radar of "real anglers'" provided big-fish excitement. We were kids at the time who fished live or dead bait and marabou jigs. It would be years until I discovered that some cattail-rimmed roadways were different.

I recall driving south to Miami in my parents' Chevy—I was maybe 13 at the time—via US 1 (aka Federal Highway). It was the only, albeit circuitous, way to get to Naples, where they had booked a weeklong golf outing. Back then, no other roads crossed the Glades. My parents' plan was to hook up with SW Eighth Street, which once it left Miami became the Tamiami Trail—a two-lane road that was only completed in the late 1920s in an effort to stimulate commerce between Tampa and Miami.

After hours of staring at uninterrupted vistas—pines, wall-to-wall mangroves, and windrows of cattails—I was ready to scream. "How much longer?" I pleaded, weak from boredom. Yet the next time I beheld this inscrutable wilderness—30 years later—I was holding a fly rod and transfixed by its beauty.

Snowy egrets gather by the thousands in winter to feed and breed in the vicinity of salt marsh puddles. PAT FORD PHOTO

The Tamiami Trail offers up endless vistas of saw grass and hardwood hammocks. Little has changed in the years since I first saw this wilderness.

Ocean piers like this one evoke the author's earliest fishing memories. They bring true deep-sea denizens within reach of shore-bound anglers. PAT FORD PHOTO

The author hefts a snook he caught and released below a water management spillway. The best fishing takes place after freshwater releases.

Massive freshwater releases from Lake Okeechobee threaten southern Florida's saltwater ecosystem. The problem has recently become more widespread. MIKE CONNER PHOTO

The author slugs it out with a roadside tarpon. Time of day isn't always an issue, while tidal phase and movement are a different story.

Plus, I'd just come nose to nose with my very first salt marsh! Though I loved the ocean and the excitement it offered, I fell head over heels for Florida's mysterious backwaters—unsullied by development—with their own set of rules and riddles. This all played out nicely with my budding interest in fly fishing—and tying—that hit me full bore by my early 20s. If I only knew then what I've learned in the meantime . . . Still, what could have replaced the wonder—the thrill of discovery—as I stood poised on the brink of exploration?

I recall my very first whiff of a sodden mudflat and the squawks of the wading birds, as well as my frustration at the hundreds, if not thousands, of snook that refused my offerings. Surely, some day I'd conjure up something to break the curse—or so I hoped. Eventually, I managed to solve a few riddles—tie a few patterns that turned the tide for me—but not overnight and not all at once. Yet aren't the sweetest of victories the ones we work for the hardest? The challenge continues and even now, decades later, I'm still that wide-eyed kid who's inching forward on a lifetime journey. Hopefully, the patterns contained here will ease your transition.

The misconception still persists among anglers in the Sunshine State, as well as the out-of-staters who come here to join us, that any fly fishing worth doing is confined to hard-to-reach mangrove shorelines, remote ocean flats that are typically accessed by skiff or kayak, or lonely beaches that remain the bailiwick of local "insiders." We've all heard that malarkey. But exciting alternatives *do* exist along Florida's southern periphery: venues like the salt marsh where fresh and salt waters meet—places where the salinity changes according to the dictates of rainfall and tide. Then, what

Katherine Linville with her bank-caught butterfly peacock—her first. She and her husband own a Key West fly shop.

The author's bug box displays popular colors. He believes in "matching the hatch" according to what's on the water.

about those nearly 1.5 million acres of meandering Everglades that I've already mentioned, or the miles of canals that transect our suburbs? Or easily reachable saltwater flats and mud banks? Or, for stay-at-home types, our endless miles of public beaches?

Fly fishers, for the most part, are aware of bonefish, tarpon, redfish, and permit hot spots, all of which are primarily skiff fisheries. Yet few realize the number—let alone the variety—of gamefish that can be accessed by walking or wading just yards from a major roadway or suburban street or parking lot. Not only do we have some of the world's finest freshwater fishing, but what awaits in the salt marsh—as well as in our inland waterways, and a short cast off our beaches—is second to none when it comes to excitement. All things considered, ours is a fly fisher's paradise.

Each region—be it fresh water; brackish salt marsh; suburban, either brackish or salty; mud bank, flat, or bay; or even the surf—has special requirements, ones uniquely suited to its particular environment. What specific forage do its predators feed on? Is forage present dependent on time of year or stage of tide—or something I've failed to mention? Here's a clue: It probably has something to do with the size of the forage—which is also affected by seasonal fluctuations.

Baitfish, like gamefish, grow as the season progresses. And lest we forget, predators change their diets as the spectrum of forage keeps unfolding. It's

The simplistic Rivet fly helped the author survive off the salt marsh. It was named for the rivets that hold the roadside siding together.

Marty Arostegui hefts a fly-caught largemouth. Bass, like most freshwater species, are more accessible during low-water periods. MARTY AROSTEGUI PHOTO

basically a matter of conserving calories. Easier to catch and more nutritious invariably walks off with the prize. Keep in mind, however, that we also have drought and rainy seasons—and that falling water goes hand in hand with our best inland fishing. Taken together, these variables control what South Florida has to offer and affect fish behavior all the way to the ocean. And who would know this better than a former walk-in guide and professional fly tier—jokingly nicknamed the "Landcaptain"—who spent more than half a lifetime sampling these venues?

I've organized this book according to the regions I mentioned. Let's start with the Everglades: Man has encroached on what remains of one of the world's last truly great wetlands for over a century, without delivering a definitive death blow. That, above all, underscores the resilience of this eons-old redoubt that refuses to succumb to pollution or draglines. The Everglades region—marked by freshwater marshes, as well as saw grass and cattail prairies—is transected by several man-made canals. Native largemouth bass, panfish, and, lately, exotic species flourish in this fluid environment that offers some of the world's best fishing with topwater lures.

Imagine a balmy day in March or April. You're paddling along in a roadside canal just off the Alligator Alley section of I-95. Although the sun's in your face, you're "keeping your cool." While the temperature remains tolerable, there

A tiny tarpon jumps in a salt marsh clearing—a familiar sight near salt marsh highways.

are no bugs to speak of and the humidity is holding. Meanwhile, the shoreline vegetation is pulsing from the reverberations of a thousand feeding bass and panfish. How intense is the action? Your bass bug disappears the second it touches the water. What follows are several hours of nonstop action that cares not a lick for the hour, nor the occasional passage of other boaters. You can get there on foot—either at docks, on the bank, or at launch ramps, but a canoe or skiff allows you to cover more water. This annual bacchanal persists until summer rains flood the marshes to overflowing, and fish quit the canals and return to the weedy morass.

Next comes the salt marsh—a low-salt brackish environment that stretches from slightly west of Ochopee, on US Highway 41, to just east of Naples—which, although you won't find it listed per se on road maps, serves up selective fishing for both salt- and freshwater gamefish, often in the same location: Hook a largemouth on one cast, a snook on the next one. In this several-mile-wide apron of cattails and mangroves that parallels at least three two-lane highways, seagoing snook, tarpon, jacks, and redfish feed alongside freshwater bass and bluegills. What makes the fishing so special? Tiny, abundant forage that makes for selective feeding.

Then, what about South Florida's myriad coastal, sea-walled waterways? First, let's make a distinction between those near inlets, which are primarily salty—the Intracoastal Waterway (ICW), Biscayne Bay, Lake Worth Lagoon (LWL), the inner bays of the Gulf—and those farther inland: ones that course through the suburbs. Of course, there's always overlap. I live on a small tidal river that changes allegiance according to rainfall. In it, I've caught everything from tarpon to grass carp—and even mullet—and all on flies. The fish in this, and similar, waterways live among us in close contiguity. It's in these suburban warrens, either brackish or fresh, that wary predators require kid-glove treatment—which they receive in a whole separate section.

Sandwiched into the freshwater portions of these waterways, along with lakes they connect with that ultimately join the Glades to the Intracoastal, are robust populations of several colorful exotics. These fish deserve—and receive—special mention.

Then, think about all those saltwater bays, along with their sea grass and mudflats—as well as their docks and catwalks—where many sought-after species can still be reached by walk-in or wading casters. These are the warrens of snook and seatrout, interspersed with an occasional tarpon and redfish. Oversize jacks crevalles roam the seawalls, while both pompano and bluefish fan out over shallow shell flats. Since this book is directed toward the shore-based angler, I have deliberately avoided patterns that are typically assigned to the big-water

Today's fly fishers target more elusive prey, like this Florida pompano. Short, Clouser-style flies—especially those tied with synthetics—are standard ammunition. PAT FORD PHOTO

Large snook cruise the South Florida surf during summer. These fish, which may be present in schools, respond to well-placed streamers. PAT FORD PHOTO

skiff crowd—with a few exceptions. Many fine books list patterns that fly fishers turn to when poling the flats or fishing offshore.

I continue my quest at our beaches, where fly fishers use specialized gear and methods to pursue a wide variety of species, including snook, bluefish, and Spanish mackerel in season—while the looming specter of giant tarpon, huge jacks, and schools of fly-snapping sharks lifts its head. The action peaks during migrations of both bait and game fish.

A current trickles through a small salt marsh culvert. Snook hide amid the roots in tiny mangrove pockets.

Then, in the final section, I move on to the true ocean flats and mud banks: the home of bonefish, redfish, permit, and tarpon. It's here, where miles of salty shallows yield to the sea, that sight-fishing reaches its finest hour. Just as it's here that mangrove islands help replenish the shortfall.

In this brief introduction I hope to convey the magic of this watery landscape—excluding its overdeveloped periphery—that flows from Lake Okeechobee, and ultimately the Kissimmee River, toward Florida Bay and the sea. Our future fishing depends on the health of this region. It's a place of dark waters that guard their secrets.

Much has changed since I first stepped onto that wilderness highway. We now face polluted runoff and water-management issues unlike any I've dealt with. Lake Okeechobee is nearing record levels, with its algae-rich excess pouring out into both the St. Lucie and Caloosahatchee Rivers. Sea grass is dying, while the headlines hover precipitously between Armageddon and "it's all part of a cycle." So what do I see as the future for our beleaguered resources?

The news, in one sense, is optimistic. Despite all the doom and gloom—including die-offs, changing salinity, possible oil exploration in the Glades, and the eternal specter of additional development—I dare to remain hopeful. Much of our backwater fishery may well dodge the bullet, while voters focus attention on these growing problems. As far as the fishing? Some species that live here will make the adjustment, so I remind the naysayers that it's a double-edged sword. By the time you read this, our inland fisheries may be South Florida's worst- or best-kept secret. Then, consider that our ocean beaches, along with parts of Biscayne Bay, the Indian River Lagoon, and even Florida Bay, may already be on the road to recovery.

Maybe that's why other anglers felt that this book was needed—not only as a follow-up to my *Ultimate Guide to Fishing South Florida on Foot*, but to assist a new generation of fly fishers who have turned their gaze "inward."

By writing these chapters, I hoped to spark an interest in tying and fishing these patterns—designs that helped me part the darkness—and in reliving their histories. And, lest I forget: They'll all produce under similar conditions wherever you find them—be it in a Virginia marsh or a Key West salt pond.

I wish you all good luck with your tying and fishing!

—Steve "Landcaptain" Kantner
May 2018, Fort Lauderdale, Florida

Catching huge grass carp on flies requires stealth and precision casting. This one engulfed a cork berry fly. LINDA TRAUB PHOTO

Amorous dragonflies provide whimsical relief from a fly fisher's "serious business." PAT FORD PHOTO

The Everglades

The Florida Everglades—that beleaguered sunken prairie, called by some the world's greatest wetland—once stretched from north of Lake Okeechobee to Florida Bay, until drain-and-fill efforts by agricultural and real estate interests shrunk what's left of it to a mere 1.5 million acres—half its original size. Still, it's in what's left of it that fly fishing for largemouth bass and several species of panfish enjoys its finest hour, both as far as numbers and in terms of surface action—meaning with bass bugs and poppers. Bass fishing in the Everglades remains a seasonal pursuit, with the best of it occurring during low-water periods—meaning South Florida's drought, which begins around Thanksgiving with the first winter cold snap, and continues into May with its increased thunderstorm activity.

A 12-foot gradient exists between Big Lake O (Lake Okeechobee) to the north and Florida Bay, so when more water heads south than falls from the sky, the swamps start draining. That's when gamefish forsake their homes in

The payoff. This jumping largemouth hit a hair bug. Hair bugs are fun to tie, and they're also effective—as long as they don't get waterlogged. PAT FORD PHOTO

Florida spotted gars, considered a nuisance by many, offer diversion for Everglades fly casters. Gars get more active in warmer water. PAT FORD PHOTO

Size 4 cork. My bugs typically get larger as the season progresses.

the marshes for several deepwater canals. Competition for food increases, and the fish turn their eyes upward—at which time the bacchanal begins in earnest. Gradually warming temperatures, both above and below the surface, drive this event toward its eventual conclusion: organized chaos.

The Importance of Weather

Weather—let's call it seasonal variations—sets the pace for fishing throughout the southern tip of the Florida peninsula. Actually, it's all about rainfall, and its effect is especially apparent in our inland waters, the Everglades in particular.

As far as what Floridians view as seasons, we only have two (the drought and the hydroperiod, or rainy season), and both correspond to rainfall amounts. The accompanying graph shows when the bulk of it falls. Meteorologist Jonathan Finch, of the National Storm Prediction Center (NOAA) in Dodge City, Kansas, plotted these figures from data collected from three key reporting stations—Miami, Palm Beach, and Fort Myers—over a 30-year period. Even a brief perusal illustrates that we get most of it during the summer, and that the deluge starts earlier near the East Coast than it does near the Gulf, where it tends to last longer. A typical scenario plays out like this:

Weather in the Northern Hemisphere moves from west to east. Concurrently, cool air masses that move inland from the Gulf of Mexico pick up moisture as they pass over the Everglades. When moisture-laden air warms, it rises, leading to condensation in the form of clouds. As the clouds continue rising, they morph into thunderheads that work their way further eastward. These deluge-producing monsters typically drop their moisture over both coastal and inland areas—with the bulk of it soaking South Florida's Glades and western suburbs.

Then, sometime around Thanksgiving, the deluges abate with the onset of cooler weather. That's when canals and marshes—now practically filled to

A huge storm closes in from the west on Jupiter Island. Violent storms—especially in summer—pack torrential rains, high winds, and the ever-present danger of lightning.

CAPTAIN CARL BALL PHOTO

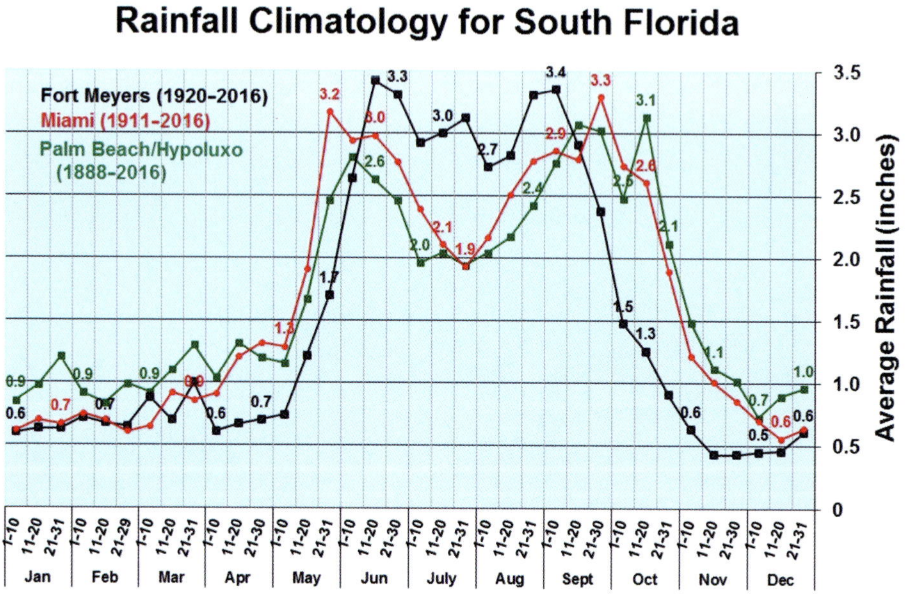

Finch's rainfall graph was plotted based on data collected from three key reporting stations.

JONATHAN FINCH PHOTO

overflowing—begin to empty as a result of "sheet flow": gravitationally induced natural drainage that results from that 12-foot gradient that exists between Lake Okeechobee and Florida Bay. Later, usually not long after New Year's, the fishing cranks up as the marshes and canals continue to empty. The action typically moves from north to south, due to the gradient. Fishing for trophy spawning, or "bedding," largemouth bass—which depends not just on water levels in the marshes—typically improves during full moon periods.

So, how do seasonal changes affect fly fishing in general? Since a fly is only effective if fish can see it, an angler's odds increase exponentially when the water drops. That's also when fish in a body of water respond to the more crowded conditions. Competition increases, and anglers are more likely to witness visible feeding. This also lets them choose between patterns—and if neither suffices, explore other options.

A prime example takes place from late winter through May—our drought—when levels in inland waters reach their lowest.

A secondary effect of seasonal variations is the temperature drop that accompanies winter. As inland waters cool, they're able to carry more dissolved oxygen, which ramps up the fishes' metabolisms and stimulates more aggressive feeding.

So, are other factors at play here? How about the reduced light intensity from a sun that, during winter, hangs lower in the sky? Remember, surface feeding typically

Salt marsh prairie during late winter—in other words, drought conditions. Compare this to the image of the same location at the end of the rainy season.

Salt marsh flat at the end of the rainy season. Note all the standing water.

takes place under low-light—as well as low-water—conditions. Figure less distance to rise and less glare to confuse. This is similar to what happens when the water turns cloudy, which goes hand in hand with low-water runoff. Did someone mention poppers? Need more persuasion to make the connection between seasons and patterns? How's this for a reason? Consistent, low-water fishing encourages casting toward banks or shoreline obstructions: a solid inducement for adding a weed guard.

Time marches on. As the drought winds to a close and waters start rising—this all coincides with the onset of thunderstorms—fish in canals disperse into marshes, where they're tougher to locate. The all-too-familiar appearance of ominous storm clouds signals the shutdown. Until the cycle repeats itself, patterns that perform well in moving water—for example, below spillways or sluices—are hands-down favorites, not only in swamps and salt creeks but also in suburban canals.

Temperature, as always, plays a role in the shift, as tarpon and exotics replace snook and bass as go-to species as the water warms. Along with the chapters, sections, and sidebars that follow, you'll find proven patterns for different species, along with descriptions of when and how to use them. ■

How good does the action get when levels bottom out? Well, hit it just right—even at midday—and several-hundred-fish excursions are not uncommon. Don't believe all the hype, though. While the majority of largemouths hug canal edges, they're not always lurking in thick vegetation. The same holds true in the marshes. Sometimes a barren bank that disguises a drop-off will hide schooling fish that are constantly moving. Finally, the summer rains fall, swelling the marshes, and the carnage subsides until the following winter, when the process repeats itself. Meteorologists see South Florida as having only two true seasons: the first, or "hydroperiod," when we receive nearly two-thirds of our annual precipitation, and the second, or "drought," which lasts from fall through late spring.

A drought in Florida? That's right, and it's when monthly rainfall amounts are measured in single digits. Everglades fishing, as well as that in the adjoining marshes—and continuing downstream all the way to the salt marsh and coastal suburbs—hits its peak during this low-water period.

Bass Bugs and Other Floating Flies

To anyone who fly-fishes locally, the cupped-face bass bug, or "popper," is the official "lure" of the Florida Everglades. Although originally designed to tempt Ozark and Appalachian smallmouths, poppers have proven equally effective for Everglades largemouths, bluegills, other assorted panfish, even gars and mudfish—and more recently, exotics. A well-made bass bug, now standard fare for fly fishers everywhere, is a thing of beauty.

Picture paddling against the backdrop of an Everglades sunset, while swirls erupt around you amidst windrows of bonnets. Or the crashing explosion when

Bass flies of every description. Often one outperforms all the others. Here, colorful "hard" and hair bugs compete with streamers for both the bass's and angler's attention.

PAT FORD PHOTO

a really big bass inhales your popper and yanks your fly line through your trembling fingers. Yet popping is more about puzzles than it is about pictures—and tapping into an environment that lies shrouded in mystery. Take how, sometimes, the fish want their bugs served up slowly—or allowed to lie motionless—then conditions change and they want something faster.

I suppose if bass were hungry enough, they'd grab a strip of banana peel, but experienced anglers know they can be very discerning at times and require

Jon Cave hoists a hefty St. Johns River largemouth. Jon's an expert on bass bugs. While naysayers see largemouths as insatiable gluttons, others (me included) insist that it's quite the opposite. One thing for sure is that for bass, size does matter—and, as I'm led to believe, so does color.

IAN SASSO PHOTO

"matching the hatch"—or choosing colors that show up under different light conditions or degrees of water clarity. The most popular in the Everglades and the surrounding marshes are pearl (baitfish), one of expert Jon Cave's favorites; basic black (cloudy water or late afternoon); gray (hazy days); robin's egg blue and so-called carrot (both dragonfly colors); and my all-around favorite, chartreuse.

I met Jon Cave at a sporting goods show, back in the days when I first started guiding. A fly-casting instructor and former guide, Jon is also a bass-buggin' fool. He's one of a vanishing breed that sees the whole enchilada—the solitude and hunting, not just racking up numbers. When I first accepted this assignment, you can guess whom I called.

It took us no time to renew our acquaintance. The first thing we agreed on was what bugs represent, and how dragonflies and damselflies—two related species—must play a major role in a largemouth's diet, not only in Central Florida where Cave fishes but here in the Everglades, both as nymphs and adults. We see dragons hovering over the water, and as the weeks go by, one species (and color) gives way to another. We'd both watched bass go airborne in pursuit of fledgling adult damsels that emerge on grass stalks—clearing the water by a yard or more in an effort to catch one.

Small fish also rank high on the menu, and bass can become very selective to size and color. When questioned about color, Jon remained emphatic on the subject of baitfish. "I mean, if they're chasing small ordinary baitfish and the bug has no white [or pearl] in it, they simply won't hit it. Same goes for matching sizes," he insisted. As far as other forage that bass bugs allegedly mimic, you're probably familiar with the usual suspects: lizards, frogs, snakes, and, lest we

Wonder what a bass sees in a bass bug? Consider that dragonflies (and their nymphs)—which are always abundant—are a major source of protein.

A well-tied deer hair damsel. Innovative tiers keep raising the bar.

A hard foam pencil popper. Notice the lack of legs. This, basically, imitates baitfish.

forget, the ubiquitous bumblebee (although I've never really seen one near the water). But "bumblebugs" work, so there must be something to it.

Regardless of what poppers represent, all should display the proportion and balance of a well-made dry fly. First comes establishing the correct proportions. I include variations with specific patterns. However, it generally comes down to this: tail = 1½ to 2 times body length; hackle = 1½ times hook gape; legs = 2

Bass prey on tiny, colorful cichlids in Glades canals. With each passing year, the menu grows larger. THE STATE OF FLORIDA'S NON-NATIVE LABORATORY PHOTO

Tiny gambusia minnows, common in roadside ditches, are a major food item for brackish and freshwater predators. KELLY GESTRING AT FLORIDA'S NON-NATIVE LABORATORY PHOTO

times length of tail. Next comes choosing the best materials: good cork or foam, or whatever you're using for bodies; the right hair and flash; and top-quality legs.

Still, I build bugs to a higher standard—making them more fun to fish with and assuring that they hold up better. As far as keeping bugs in good working order, I've learned to never grab the body while unhooking a fish. That breaks

The late Jack "Bass" Allen, archetypical Everglades fly guide, remains a legend in the minds of many. Jack led his customers to triple-digit catches with "styrobugs"—poppers he crafted from unpainted Styrofoam fishing floats. Styrofoam's major drawback lies in the fact that, in Jack's words, "it's only slightly more durable than popcorn."

the hook loose internally and allows it to spin—usually creating a "fishless" bug. Grab the hook bend instead. The wreckage caused by this gaffe can sometimes be repaired by tearing out the hook and gluing it back anew—once you get home.

This leads to a story on the subject of legs, which most bugs come equipped with. Here's how Jack Allen told it:

> I once fished with a friend in Monet, Missouri, who tied bugs professionally. He'd tell me stories about the local farm ponds, and how one guy in particular, who wasn't a customer, came in to report that he'd just raised a monster—mind you, on three consecutive casts—without getting "the hit." All he got for his efforts was a massive boil that sucked at the surface before disappearing. The guy's legs were still shaking when my friend asked him the operative question—one concerning his popper.
>
> "But did it have legs? If only it had legs."
>
> Case closed.

A chartreuse cork bass bug, the quintessential Everglades standard. The author has probably caught more bass on this lure—and color—than all others combined.

Cork frog. Both cork and balsa encourage tiers' creativity.

Meanwhile, bass bugs are distinguished by more than just color. Some are fully dressed, while others such as pencil poppers are tied sparsely to imitate baitfish. Poppers come in all shapes and sizes

In summary, I've fished bugs of all sizes and descriptions. While small double-tapered or "hourglass" corks were popular during the "lean" 1980s, revised limits have increased the size of our Everglades bass. Now I seldom go smaller than a size 6, or even a size 4 as the season progresses. Then, by mid-June, I'll switch to a giant hair bug.

CONSTRUCTING CORK POPPERS

Making bass bugs is rewarding, as well as cost-effective. While the process takes time to master, proficiency comes faster than it does with, say, upright hair-wing dry flies or feather-wing streamers. When it comes to bodies—the tapered, cupped variety—I prefer cork hands down. Cork floats high, it's durable, and it's easy to work with. And, as of the time of this writing, it's still available in preformed bodies.

Behold the ubiquitous bumblebee! "Bumblebugs" work, although the author has yet to see a natural on the water. MARTY AROSTEGUI PHOTO

Building bugs is more "heavy construction" than actual tying. As I learned long ago from the late master Bob Kay, making good-looking bugs requires organization as well as practice. Bob, incidentally, was the first to "officially" standardize tarpon flies, but that's another story. However, he's best remembered for his encyclopedic knowledge of largemouth bass and the lures that tempt them. To make optimal use of his time, Bob assembled his favorites—slotted tapered cork bugs—in three distinct stages: During the initial setup, he glued, painted, and gloss-coated the bodies. In the second stage, he added tails and hackles. Then, in the final stage, he sewed in the legs and added a weed guard.

Stage 1

Like Bob, I'll gather a dozen Gamakatsu SS15 hooks on the desk before me. I prefer size 4s, but that's a bit subjective. While I occasionally match the hook to the exact matching cork size, I typically choose hooks that are one size larger. Next, I'll spread out a handful of tapered, slotted corks and check them out for any obvious defects. If possible, I use whatever comes in the package. I'll clean

them up as well as possible—with a file and 400-grit sandpaper—and discard any hopeless cases. I pay especially close attention to the lip, where the "pop" originates.

After prepping the bodies, I'm ready to glue in the hooks. To that end, I either mix up a dollop of 5-minute epoxy—having had my fill of old-style cyanoacrylates that need pressure to bond and are a pain to work with—or use Loctite Super Glue Gel Control (it comes in a gray bottle). Here's a tip when gluing: Quit wrapping the hook shanks with tying thread, since both adhesives stick just fine to plain old metal. Instead, slop the mixed two-part epoxy directly on the hook shank before forcing it into the precut slot. With Loctite, I do just the opposite, by running a bead down the slot before forcing the shank into it.

I then set the bodies aside to dry—taking care to maintain the proper hook/body alignment. I try to keep glue out of hook eyes, so before I get started, I give each slot a lick with a sharp-edged file to make positioning the hook that much easier, and avoid the problem. If I'm using epoxy, after it sets, I check for drips and runs, which I file away. Then, after it hardens I'm ready to paint.

Stage 2

I begin Stage Two by coating the bodies with gesso (available at art supply shops). For those of you who aren't art majors, gesso is an acrylic medium that artists use to paint white backgrounds on their canvasses before starting their works in earnest. Think of it as creative primer. Fortunately, since acrylics are

water-based, your tying area needn't smell like a body shop. And since acrylics dry quickly, the process is fast and relatively painless. Once the gesso dries, I brush on a single coat of whatever color acrylic (also available at arts-and-crafts shops) I'm planning on using. When that dries, I use different-size nail heads—or sawed-off paintbrush handles—to apply eyes and decorative dots that both bass and bass fishermen love so well. This photo shows the completed body in vise. At this point, you're done with the painting.

One of my favorite combinations is a chartreuse body covered with black dots, but for the coup de grâce, I paint a red bull's-eye with a black center smack-dab on the bottom. If I have time, I'll create three-color eyes by dabbing sequentially with different-size nail or pin heads, or the sawed-off handles of paintbrushes. (I wait for each application to dry before adding the next. For example, I might make eyes by following red with white, and then black.)

Don't forget: Every time acrylic dries, any unwashed "applicator" gets a wee bit larger.

Finally, after the body has dried completely, I apply one or more coats of gloss. I used to use glaze, but due to a number of drawbacks, I needed a better alternative—which I had no trouble finding. I now use a translucent acrylic that goes on cloudy before drying clear without fumes or mess. The Liquitex folks call it an acrylic "varnish." Look for it at arts-and-crafts shops, where you bought the gesso. You can clean your brush afterward with ordinary tap water.

However, say you haven't gotten the word yet and you're still working with glaze. Bugs coated with newly applied glaze—ones that you might think are dry—tend to stick together if they come in contact. So wait several days before moving any fledglings into your fly box.

To complete Stage Two, I tie in the legs, flash, tail, and hackle.

I begin by clamping each assembled body back in my vise and covering the quarter-inch or so of hook shank that lies directly behind it with tying thread. Next, I use the thread to anchor three or four strands of rubber leg material against the body before stretching them back toward the rear. While stretching the legs, I bind the butts down with additional thread wraps, so when I ease off on the pressure and the rubber relaxes, they're literally locked in place.

After tying in the legs, I'm ready to add the flash, tail, and hackle. First, I tie in the flash. Due to its resilience, and since I'm not looking for "flex," I prefer Krystal Flash—less is more here. After adding the flash, I tie on the tail, which consists of a medium-size pinch of dyed squirrel tail, stacked and measured at

a length equal to one-and-a-half times that of the body. I consider these proportions standard when making a bass bug. Then, once you've secured the wing, tear off the Krystal Flash directly behind the hair.

Now you're ready to add the hackle. Start out by selecting a feather, either a saddle or neck, that's slightly darker than, or that contrasts with, the body. I prefer soft-fibered feathers with lots of webbing. Size isn't that important, but it helps to keep things in proportion. According to one old rule, the flues should average one-and-a-quarter times the hook gape. Before tying in the hackle, I bring the thread back to the rear of my previous wraps. I tie in the hackle tip-first, while keeping the concave side facing the rear. Now, I bend it forward before winding the tying thread to a point next to the body. I let the bobbin hang there while I saturate the thread wraps with head cement.

An inexpensive, dyed grizzly hen neck is perfect for making bug hackles—the webbier, the better—but so is a webby saddle. Before the head cement dries, I wind the hackle through it and tie off the butt directly behind the body. Before whip-finishing the thread, I take a few serpentine wraps through the hackle (being careful not to crush the barbs). This locks the stem in place.

Hackle and tail in place.

Stage 3

Now it's on to Stage Three, where I sew in the legs and weed guard.

Rubber strips, hard mono, bodkin, and home-made threader: All are needed to sew in legs and a mono horseshoe weed guard.

You'll need specialized tools in order to sew in the legs and weed guard. The first of these, an ordinary bodkin, must be both stiff and sharp, since you'll be

forcing it through the body. The second, a modified bobbin-threader, has to be thin in order to pass through the hole created by the bodkin. You can make your own threader by epoxying a short loop of No. 2 leader wire into a drilled glass bead. When you form the loop, pinch it as tight as possible with pliers.

Sewing in the legs is the fun part. Start by making two crisscrossing holes in the cork body at the approximate midpoint (above the hook shank). Use caution while pushing! After punching the holes, work the threader through the body and use the wire loop to catch the tip of each rubber leg. Afterward, carefully pull it through the body and adjust the length with your fingers. (It helps if you moisten the rubber legs with saliva before beginning this process.) But here, I force the bodkin upward and slightly forward, and instead of threading rubber leg material, I pull a length of Mason's 10-pound-test hard mono down first, then upward, to form a horseshoe-shaped loop at the bottom. After snugging the loop to the body, I touch both free ends of the mono (at the top of the bug) with a drop of Loctite before pulling them down with the bodkin, thereby enlarging the loop—which pulls the glue and mono into the body, where the weed guard is now locked firmly in place.

The bug is complete now, weed guard and all. I consider weed guards essential for nearly all bass applications. I seldom see weed guards on commercially

tied bugs, which, quite frankly, confounds me. You might have to add one yourself—especially since largemouths lurk in or near cover, making protection essential for Everglades fishing.

The bug as seen from above. Notice what bug experts call the "foot pattern." While weed guards are important, they shouldn't interfere with a bug's hooking ability, so make sure your hook point has plenty of clearance.

Closed-Cell Foam Patterns

Closed-cell foams, although relatively new on the market, offer a high-tech adjunct to the natural alternative. Let's start with Styrofoam, a proprietary product developed by Dow Chemical back in the 1940s.

Styrofoam, which is extruded from polystyrene, is used for insulation as well as craft applications—among them, bug-making. Bug tiers note: Styrofoam makes state-of-the-art bodies, but be prepared to assemble huge quantities, due to the material's lack of durability. Old-style cyanoacrylates react with Styrofoam, making it melt on contact. Jack Allen recommended Loctite Super Glue Gel Control. He claimed it's better for gluing in mono weed guards (see the preceding bass bug section) than other adhesives.

Foams are currently available in various degrees of hardness, colors, and shapes, including cylinders that can easily be trimmed to size. Other closed-cell foam products include various prefab soft, squishy bodies (they come in assorted sizes and colors); tiny spider bodies; and those rock-hard blanks that a shark couldn't ding. I use skinny versions of the hard stuff for pencil poppers. Prefab bodies are usually sold in kits that include a supply of hump-shank hooks. While these hooks pass muster for light freshwater work, they're way too flimsy for snook and tarpon and for heavier tippets, which are typically associated with salt marsh fishing.

Styrofoam bugs in one of the author's fly boxes.

Cup-faced strip foam popper. The possibilities with foam are endless.

Foam—both open and closed-cell—is now available in precut or molded cylinders. Tiers can choose from a wide selection.

For the salt, use a standard saltwater long-shank such as a Mustad 34011. The only problem, and it's not insurmountable, is fitting the thicker shank into a slot designed for a much thinner hook. I used to waste time in the beginning with a file and sandpaper (remember, this foam is hard and unforgiving), until it finally dawned on me: Heat the hook with a "torch" cigar lighter, then plunge it into the slot.

Bob's Banger

- **Hook:** #2/0–4/0 Mustad 34011
- **Thread:** White 6/0 or 140-denier
- **Tail:** White bucktail
- **Adhesive:** Zap-A-Gap
- **Midsection:** Gold Estaz or Cactus Chenille
- **Head:** Wapsi Foam Cylinder, 1/2-inch diameter cut in half to save weight and material
- **Head covering:** Yellow Fish Scale Witchcraft Tape
- **Eyes:** 1/2-inch prismatic silver Witchcraft Tape Flat Lure Eyes

Bob's Banger is a popular synthetic popper designed by New Jersey tier Bob Popovics. Ease of construction makes a big difference—especially when fishing for rugged saltwater species. Use a bodkin to punch a hole lengthwise through both ends of the foam. When the hole is centered, heat up the bodkin and repeat the process.

Grip the hook with pliers while you heat the shank to a dull red color. Once the hook is set in place and properly aligned, set the body aside to cool. Then, after the plastic has hardened, fill in the slot with epoxy or superglue. Finally, lay down a few thread wraps just ahead of the hook bend and add a short tail (see photo) after stacking a hank of superfine bucktail—or if targeting sharp-toothed species, Ultra Hair. Since I'm trying to imitate baitfish, I don't bother painting the bodies (they're pearl-white to begin with). However, adding a few strands of Krystal Flash is always an option.

JACK GARTSIDE'S GURGLER

Jack Gartside, a Harvard graduate and Boston cabbie, earned a reputation for his many fly-tying innovations. He was, from all accounts, an enigma, as well as a minimalistic but effective tier. His Gurgler (a variation of a popper) ranks among the most famous patterns, and I always have a few variations of it in my box.

Gartside's Gurgler (Jody Moore's version)

- **Hook:** #1/0 Mustad 34007
- **Thread:** Clear mono, or a color that matches the foam strip, wrapped the entire shank from the hook bend to the eye before adding materials
- **Tail:** 1 1/2-inch length of bucktail
- **Shellback:** Tapered white foam strip less than 1/4 inch wide, tied in first over the base of the tail and later at the hook eye
- **Body:** Pearl Krystal Flash, wrapped forward
- **Hackle:** Neck hackle palmered forward, butt first with the flues facing backward, tied off at the hook eye after tying off the Krystal Flash. Trim the flues on top so the shellback hugs the body, then tie off the foam strip just behind the hook eye.

Gartside's Gurgler. Jack Gartside—acknowledged as a tier and innovator—wrote several books on fly tying. This most basic of poppers (Gartside called them "surface flies") can be assembled in practically no time from a flat strip of foam, a wisp of bucktail, wound hackle, and a Crystal Chenille body. It's a great fly to cast into the shadows of mangrove overhangs, around fall-downs, and on the up-tide side of oyster bars, as well as shoreline points and other ambush spots—or even on the open when the sun is low.

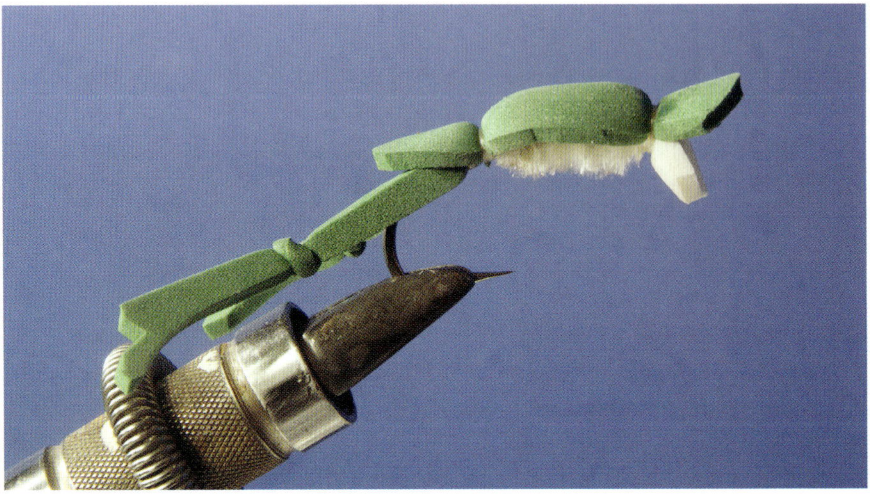

A foam-strip frog—in some ways, similar to Gartside's Gurgler.

- **Gills (optional):** Small tufts of red marabou, tied slightly behind and beneath the hook eye
- **Note:** The palmered hackle can act as a weed guard, giving a snag-free effect to your fly, which is another attribute of this pattern. That is why it is not necessary to tie on a weed guard for this pattern, assuming you don't trim the hackle so short as to expose the hook point.

Local angler/tier Richard J. "Jody" Moore has amassed a wealth of knowledge fishing South Florida's mangrove backwaters—both from the bank and his flats skiff. He considers the Gurgler an all-purpose fly (his favorite color is white) that is essential for every saltwater box. According to Jody, "Being a surface fly, it's not so much a pattern for *every* condition, as one to be used on relatively calm days. It's more effective when it's fished under low-light conditions, like at the start or end of the day—when fish are more likely to be feeding on top."

The Gurgler is quick and easy to tie, and imitates a broad range of surface foods. Jody continued:

> Given its thin profile, length, and palmered hackle, I tie my Gurglers to imitate shrimp. I believe the sparse bucktail tail mimics a shrimp's antennae. You can add plastic black barbell eyes to either end, if you prefer more of a shrimp look. While fish like redfish, snook, and seatrout eat shrimp—and I catch them on Gurglers—this pattern could just as easily appear as a wounded minnow. While the buoyancy of the foam keeps the fly floating,

it's the signature flange at the front that creates the action when the fly is pulled along the surface with short, fast strips. That causes it to push and spray water—which, in turn, creates a small surface disturbance and sound—hence the name, Gurgler.

MARTY AROSTEGUI'S UNSINKABLE FROG

Marty Arostegui ties most of the flies he uses to catch his world records—of which there are many—so when he sits at the vise, he knows where he's headed. In addition to fishing the world with well-known guides, Marty's a do-it-yourselfer—a guy who spends hours fishing both the Glades and his local suburbs. What he wanted most when he dreamt up this pattern was a fly that showed plenty of bulk while making a significant surface impression—something to bring up a bass or a snakehead—in short, a fat, unsinkable frog.

Marty's Unsinkable Frog

- **Hook:** #3/0 Gamakatsu SB11-3L3H
- **Thread:** Green chartreuse Danville's flat waxed nylon
- **Weed guard:** A short length of 20-pound Mason's hard mono
- **Body:** Chartreuse and dark brown 2mm foam sheets
- **Tail:** Chartreuse bucktail
- **Flash:** Pearl or chartreuse Krystal Flash
- **Hackle:** None. A short length of red flash or fuzz that extends from the sides of the body makes this fly more appealing.
- **Eyes:** Hollow doll's eyes
- **Dots:** Black inside red, applied with a colored permanent marker

Tying Marty Arostegui's Frog:

1. Start by tying in a length of 20-pound Mason's hard mono at the hook bend, using your tying thread. This is the start of your weed guard. Add a length of bucktail and flash—approximately two times the body length—over the top of the mono. Then, bring your tying thread forward to just short of the hook eye.

2. Cut a chartreuse foam strip approximately 5/8 inch wide and 3 inches long, and attach facing forward slightly behind the hook eye.

3. Coat the strip with superglue and roll it tightly upward before tying it off, forming a tiny, rolling pin–shaped head. Trim the excess to approximately 1 1/4 inches.

4. Snip a wedge-shaped cut in the foam behind where you just tied it in before gluing the strip back onto itself, after inserting and gluing a short strip of brown foam, which, like the chartreuse foam, you'll roll upward and forward.

Marty Arostegui's frog is tied to create a big disturbance and bring bullseye snakeheads running. It's also effective on suburban largemouths. MARTY AROSTEGUI PHOTO

5. At this point you may wish to add a short length of red material—say, a hunk of flash or fuzz—inside the loop, so that it protrudes from both sides of the body.
6. Bring the chartreuse foam forward and tie it down (where you cut the wedge) at the approximate point where you originally started. Glue on the doll's eyes.
7. Tie in the front of the weed guard just behind the hook eye, making sure there's plenty of clearance, and tie off your thread.
8. Dot the body with a permanent marker. Marty's (and my) favorite? Red dots with black centers.

THE FINISHED MINNOW

So there I sit, paddling a canoe down a lonely canal that borders Alligator Alley. It's late afternoon a day or two after Valentine's Day, and I'm the only one out there—until I discover a guy in a tin boat who's casting a floating Rapala. As I close the distance between us, I can't help noticing what he's doing.

It looks like he's anchored at the edge of a floating weed bed, slowly working his plug with what looks like a series of twitches—without much reeling. Finally, as I keep getting closer—and the sun dips lower—I see him pull the anchor. I then hear him hand-crank what looks, and sounds, like a 10-horse outboard and watch as he makes his way in my direction. Then, when he finally slows down alongside me (Everglades etiquette: avoid making wakes), we exchange greetings.

The Finished Minnow

- **Hook:** #6 Mustad 37187
- **Thread:** Olive Danville's flat waxed nylon or Monocord
- **Head cement:** 5-minute two-part epoxy
- **Body:** Hard, closed-cell foam, spray-painted with enamel
- **Eyes:** Painted or decal
- **Flash:** Gold Flashabou
- **Coating:** Heavy gloss coat (needs to hold the flash and eyes in place)
- **Tail:** Twin tufts of tan marabou

Tying Tips

1. Measure a hard-foam pencil popper body alongside the shank of the Mustad 37187 stinger hook. This is an extremely lightweight model, just what you want here. Allow just enough room on the shank to accommodate the angled face (as illustrated) and to attach a tail.

2. Using a hacksaw blade, cut the foam body so that the face is angled in the direction of the preformed hook groove. After forming the body, mix up a small batch of 5-minute epoxy and apply it (or Loctite Gel Control) to the hook shank before forcing the hook into the groove. It isn't necessary to wrap the shank with tying thread prior to applying the epoxy. Set the body aside to dry.

The Finished Minnow. This hard foam bug behaves more like a surface wobbler. This pattern is a bona fide "keeper."

Finished Minnows drying on a balsa block. Largemouths in South Florida gorge primarily on nondescript baitfish, especially in the spring when the water's still warming. Whereas most commercial bass bugs resemble land-based creatures, this hard-foam beauty is clearly an exception.

3. When you're sure the glue is dry, spray the body with silver enamel (available at auto parts stores). After the silver paint dries, spray the back of the bug—only this time a darker shade such as olive, brown, black, or gray. Once again, let everything dry. Wearing a pair of latex or nitrile gloves keeps your hands clean.

4. Place the painted body in your vise and attach your tying thread directly behind the body. Secure the thread in place by taking a few turns, and allow the bobbin to hang. Select several strands of gold Flashabou, and using an ordinary pin stuck in the bug face to help position it, loop the Flashabou around the pin and pull it backward along both sides of the body. Finally, tie it off at the hook bend before securing it further by pasting on decal eyes.

5. Now you're ready to coat the body with gloss coat. Be sure to cover the Flashabou and brush it on quickly. The solvents in most clear gloss products tend to "melt" enamel, thereby creating smears. After the gloss dries, use your scissors to snip away any excess Flashabou from the bug's face. Now's the time to remove the pin and paint the face with red acrylic for better visibility. Later on, you can touch up the face with a dab of gloss in order to create a chip-free finish. In applying a top coat to bugs, less is more. Too much coating destroys the bug's buoyancy and therefore its effectiveness.

6. To complete the fly, tie in a tan marabou tail over the Flashabou strands that extend beyond the body.

When the conversation turns to "So how'd ya do?" I say, "I'm just getting started." Then, as he motors away, I see his stringer. It's one of those chains with the clips—and affixed to those clips, I see two or three monsters.

I find my own weed bed and retrace his footsteps—only my surface wobbler/diver is attached to a fly rod. Time's a-wastin'—and I'm losing daylight—but I still manage to get in on the action.

My "minnow" disappears with scarcely a swirl. It's like when Mr. Creosote (of Monty Python fame) opts for that last thin mint. So, what does it mean if you see emergent weeds moving (meaning bass are bumping them), but no surface eruptions? Two more weeks of slow-twitch fishing.

Lure manufacturers aren't nearly as timid—or shall I say "traditional"—as fly tiers, meaning they do a bang-up job of imitating all manner of baitfish. Highly effective twitch baits such as the floating Rapalas can either be twitched and rested or reeled steadily in order to imitate an injured minnow. Several have earned themselves huge reputations, and one in particular might be the world's most popular lure. You know the one: It's what got me hooked on trying to re-create this effect for fly rods. I'd wondered for years if I could tweak the design, so fly fishers could keep up with the "ratchet reel set."

My Finished Minnow is just what the name infers: a baitfish imitation that wobbles like those well-known plugs—if it's properly "finished." Its decal eyes and reflective sides resemble those of the famed balsa wobbler. Call it a fly-rod plug if you must—albeit with a single hook and marabou tail. Forget the legs and goo-goo eyes and the other filigree that's associated with standard poppers! This one catches bass when the others won't—something that's partially dependent on the time of year.

Here's how it works: There's a period that, most years, lasts for several weeks. It's after the bass start feeding but when they're not ready to come up on top yet. The water's still cold. However, bass are eyeing the surface and gulping baitfish just beneath it, but since they won't break through the film yet, they won't hit a popper.

It's a time of transition, which you'll recognize the first time you see it—from the visible activity compared to the lack of hits. Try landing your popper next to all those spraying minnows. Did you get as much as a sniff? Not surprising. Okay, now try tossing them a Finished Minnow. Notice the difference? It may take a cast or two to find the retrieve they're looking for—a simple bump-and-twitch typically works for me. Keep this in mind, too: Bass grab this bug just under the surface, with barely a swirl.

The Finished Minnow's crowning glory lies in its wobble—which would be severely hampered by any extraneous fittings, like weed guards. So don't add one to this fly and instead try retrieving it alongside, rather than through, any floating weeds. You can also face-cut the Finished Minnow on a reverse bias. The idea is to tie a bug that dives and wobbles rather than pops for early-season fishing.

Balsa Basics

Balsa, like cork, is a lightweight wood that not only floats high, but has a soft consistency that makes it a pleasure to work with. It's also resilient, which—so to speak—adds to its luster. But unlike cork, it's not available commercially (not to my knowledge) in preformed bodies. This puts the onus on tiers to whittle their own.

I've used balsa for various applications. If it has any drawbacks, it's in the work that's required to shape the finished product. But there's good news here, too! Consider working with an inexpensive material that can be shaped however you want it. The possibilities are endless!

Large balsa popper. Balsa, like foam or cork, is lightweight but more resilient. To shape the head, I use a hacksaw and razor blades, a Dremel drill with a rounded bit (if I want a concave face), and at least two grades of sandpaper—starting with 60-grit and working down to around 400. For an adhesive, I prefer two-part 5-minute epoxy.

I remember carving out shapes for both fresh and salt water—but there's one in particular that sticks in my mind. Once, in a fit of creative hubris, I fashioned a "whale bug"—gray back, red mouth, and all, complete with a blowhole. The idea behind it? When popped, it would "spout" like its namesake, as well as gurgle. Naturally, after all that sweat and aggravation, I was reluctant to test it, so it lived on a shelf at the local fly shop until some scoundrel eventually scarfed it. Looking for a whale bug? I hear they're a rare commodity.

Still, balsa offers just the right "heft," as well as a look back in history. So when I want something larger and stronger than foam or cork—like a 6/0 popper to toss at the giant jack crevalles that run up and down seawalls—and a material that isn't too heavy, balsa's my choice.

TOM LOVING'S GERBUBBLE BUG

In his classic *Complete Book of Fly Fishing* (Outdoor Life, 1958 and 1968), Joe Brooks had this to say about the Gerbubble Bug:

> In my book, the all-time greatest bass bug, the one I think is a mile ahead of any other for largemouth, is the Gerbubble Bug, invented in the late 1920s by Tom Loving of Baltimore, Maryland. Because it is difficult to make, and because the pattern has seldom appeared in print, this wonderful bug is little used.

One thing you can bet on: This lure set the standard, with its low, flat profile; flexible tail; and hackles that extended out from the sides—where tiers now add rubber or silicone legs. It's still highly effective—the rules haven't changed much. Plus, it's the all-time poster child for working with balsa. Assembling Gerbubble Bugs isn't all that difficult—if you don't mind whittling and a bit of waiting.

Once, while discussing Gerbubble Bugs with Lefty Kreh (he's tied plenty), he shared a secret: "I prefer marabou for the side hackles," he told me—which only makes sense, since the filaments are longer and a lot more flexible. So now when I'm forced to use hackle, it's only the aftershaft filaments from the base of the feather.

As an added touch—because where I fish you need one—I punch two holes through the bug, into which I insert a short length of Mason's 20-pound hard mono. I add a drop of Loctite to the ends where they protrude from the back and, pushing my bodkin through the loop, use it to draw them back through the body. That's all there is to it!

Gerbubble Bug

- **Hook:** #2 Mustad 37190 light wire "stinger"
- **Thread:** Monocord, color to match body
- **Body:** Tapered balsa
- **Side hackles:** Aftershaft saddle or marabou fluff
- **Traditional hackle:** Soft webby saddle
- **Tail:** Squirrel hair or bucktail around which splayed saddles are tied
- **Weed guard:** 20-pound mono

Tying Tips

1. Saw a ½-inch-thick rectangle from a balsa block—blocks are available online or at hobby shops—or you can purchase precut strips in various thicknesses. I use a hacksaw blade for sawing and later a single-edged razor blade for cutting out bodies and making slots for the hook and two side hackles. Once you achieve the correct proportions, finish the job with medium-grit sandpaper.

2. Cut a slit for the hook, and glue the hook in place with Loctite. Coat the body with gesso before applying a coat of colored acrylic. Cut slits along each side before adding three-color eyes and black spots (my favorite), then add several coats of gloss acrylic.

Gerbubble Bug. According to Joe Brooks, Tom Loving originally tied his bugs on "a 2/0 hook with CORK (image that!) body 9/16" high, 11/16" wide and 7/8" long." I scale mine down for Everglades fishing and use marabou instead of the hackle aftershaft feather. And I start with balsa, which Loving eventually switched to.

3. After the final gloss coat dries, add a tail—a combination of hair (your choice, but I'm partial to bucktail) surrounded by a half dozen saddles—along with a soft hackle collar. I usually match feathers and glue the butts together, but here I attach them in a haphazard fashion to achieve an unkempt look—like a frog's legs. Finally, glue in the side hackles—Loving originally used schlappen—after running a dab of Loctite down each side slit. Here's a tip: Use ordinary tweezers to help insert the feathers.

Hair Bugs

I have friends who—when they're on leave from the asylum—spin deer hair so tight that we mortals can't cut it (they use X-Acto knives or double-edged razor blades when the orderlies allow them access). To purists, spun hair—be it deer, elk, or antelope—is the Holy Grail: the ultimate expression of the fly tier's art. Me? I'm into utility. I like flies that float well and are durable.

At one time or another, I've tied with all manner of hair. The softer it is—remember, we're talking the hollow stuff here—the neater the head at the expense of durability. The really delicate stuff, like coastal whitetail deer hair (great for small dry flies), is so fragile that tying thread—even the flat kind—tends to cut it, so I look for a happy medium. Remember, hair from two seemingly identical deer tails can also vary.

Old-time hair frogs fooled many a bass in their day. Back then, however, tiers didn't always have access to woods like cork or balsa—let alone Space Age materials—so it was hair or nothing. This one's known as the Bass Houn', and all I can identify for certain are the two outstretched wings. To be honest, they resemble an old-time shaving brush.

Colorful selection of hair bugs. These are either poppers, divers, or swimmers. MIKE CONNER PHOTO

Large, colorful hair bugs make a splash with tiers—but not always with fish. When a hair bug gets waterlogged, it floats low in the water, making it harder to lift, plus it casts like a seagull and won't pop or chug when you strip it. At that point you're basically out of business, so be sure to change it.

A tightly spun face makes for noisier popping. Use a commercially available or homemade "pusher" to pack it.

For the best-possible hair bugs, the trick's in the spinning. Start slowly, by making two loose thread wraps around a small bundle—its diameter depending on the thickness of the individual hairs (smaller is better but more time-consuming)—which you've placed on top of the hook shank, tips pointed backward. Remember, the shank should be bare. Slowly tighten the thread as you release the shafts that you're pinching between your thumb and forefinger. Do this correctly, and the hair flares evenly.

Next, tighten the thread and make a few additional wraps immediately ahead of where you just spun the hair. Push the wraps to the rear with an empty ballpoint pen case or a hair packer, and secure the thread with a drop of head cement. In the interest of making durable hair heads, I repeat this process between each application. For variegated bugs, I sequentially add bundles of different-colored hair of a similar consistency.

If you plan to add legs, remove the unfinished bug from your vise with the thread still attached, after making one or two whip-finishes to keep it from unraveling. Use your scissors to trim the body, then it's back to the vise. Tie in legs at the middle, splaying them sideways with X-wraps. You can trim them later. The longer they are, the farther they hang—meaning out of the way.

Temptation lands among the bonnets. Is a largemouth lurking? PAT FORD PHOTO

After forcing the thread wraps backward, keep adding additional hair clumps. Remove your unfinished bug from the vise once you've added—and compacted—enough hair to complete the pattern. Now, while holding the legs to the rear and out of the way, shape the front of the bug with your scissors. As a final precaution, coat all thread wraps—and with a flat-faced hair bug, the front—with several coats of cement.

Here's a tip if you plan to fish hair bugs: Spray them with Scotchgard, or an aerosol dry-fly spray, and allow them to dry before using. Then, when you're ready to use one, apply liquid floatant. Touch treated bugs to the surface before actually fishing—this tends to disperse any excess floatant. Just remember, once a bug becomes waterlogged, it goes back in your cooler.

THE LEGS DIAMOND

Year after year, fly fishers haul untold numbers of largemouth bass from freshwater haunts throughout the Sunshine State—from the Glades especially. Regrettably, most are "dinks." According to the experts, this "shortfall" is due primarily to the size of our lures, not some weakness in the resource. I agree wholeheartedly, so whenever practical I toss 'em something larger.

Unfortunately, when it comes to fly casting, size equates with pain. So most fly fishers are content to cast size 6 poppers and settle for ¾- to 2-pound "stud bass." If you're among them, you need read no further. But if you've ever wanted to go for the gusto, why not embrace the lightning? To jaded anglers, catching yearling bass quickly becomes boring—and who hasn't yearned for that occasional monster? Now, wouldn't it be great to lose the light stuff and do battle with a bass that could break a rod, let alone an 8-pound tippet? Well, here's how to do it:

Legs Diamond

- **Hook:** #10 Tiemco 8089
- **Thread:** Black or chartreuse Danville's flat waxed nylon
- **Weed guard:** Twin loops of 10-pound Mason's hard mono or a #2 stainless wire moustache
- **Tail:** 30 strands of "old-style" rubber, color to match the body
- **Body:** Dyed, tapered deer hair from an eastern whitetail
- **Legs:** 10–15 strands of old-style rubber, color to match the body
- **Eyes (optional):** Large hollow plastic

Tying Tips

1. After inserting the hook and wrapping a short thread base, starting at the hook bend, wrap the thread along the bend in order to bind double strands of the hard mono to either side of the shank. Be careful not to tie it too close to the hook point, or

The Legs Diamond in black, one of my two favorite colors (the other is chartreuse). The Legs Diamond is more of a waking pattern that makes no pretense of popping. What it does is bring up the biggies like few other patterns.

you won't be able to hook any fish. Afterward, pinch the mono in a hemostat and allow it to hang out of the way. Tie in approximately 30 strands of rubber leg material and soak the thread wraps with Flexament or clear nail polish.

2. Starting at the bend, spin a chartreuse or black deer hair body, making sure to pack the hair tightly and glue the thread wraps between each application. Continue spinning the deer hair until you reach approximately mid-shank. At this point, tie off the thread with a whip-finish.

3. Grip the rubber legs with a hemostat before removing the fly from the vise. With the legs out of the way, trim the rear half of the body as illustrated in the photo. After shaping the hair, trim the bottom flat in order to leave sufficient gape. Return the fly to the vise, and while crisscrossing with your thread, tie in another half-dozen rubber strands so they extend sideways from where you previously tied off the hair.

4. Continue spinning deer hair to the eye, and change colors if you wish. When finished, secure the legs by pulling them down and backward. Remove the fly from the vise and trim the body a second time before pulling the legs back into position.

5. Bring the two strands of mono through the hook eye and measure the resulting loops before binding the ends down and backward with your thread. If gauged correctly, each loop should barely protect the hook point. Finally, use Goop to glue a pair of hollow plastic eyes in place before brushing the bottom with Flexament.

More than one angler who has examined my fly box has commented on a hair bug that's the size of a well-fed tarantula. I call it the Legs Diamond, at the suggestion of former *Warmwater Fly Fishing* editor John Likakis, who came up with the name. Need I mention that it's shaped roughly like a diamond, and that it sports multiple rubber legs? While this hand-size monstrosity may resemble a fruit bat, its streamlined profile and nonabsorbent materials make it easier to cast than similar yet smaller hair bugs. When I first sat down to tie this pattern, I wanted something to tempt larger largemouths and wasn't a problem to cast. I'd like to believe that I accomplished my mission.

The materials I use to tie this pattern squeeze together when it's in the air, then splay when it lands on the water—like the proverbial bug on the windshield. Since the "Legs" absorbs little water (if it's properly greased), it's a snap to pick it up and false cast—something that makes it worth its weight in ibuprofen.

Let me say it again: When this monstrosity lands on the water, its "footprint" expands. Then, all those legs keep pumping throughout the retrieve. Together with the subtle wake, that opening and closing drives big bass nuts. If you're into poundage, this bug's for you. More than oversize poppers or subsurface swim-baits, it brings up the monsters while weeding out "dinks." I can throw

Ready for work, the Legs Diamond is about to be deployed along Alligator Alley. Fish Everglades canals from late May through June—just when the water is starting to rise—and you'll be surprised at the number of big fish you'll see if you use this pattern.

it for hours (while changing it every so often whenever it gets waterlogged) without fatigue.

I discovered the concept of rubber overkill in a photo of Kevin McEnerney's Crazy-legs Spider that appeared in Dick Stewart and Farrow Allen's excellent *Flies for Bass and Panfish* (1992). I decided on tying a larger version, with modifications. In spite of all the high-tech materials that are currently available, I prefer old-style rubber legs—for durability. I added a double mono or wire moustache weed guard and experimented with hooks, before adding hollow eyes. I eventually settled on the current pattern. While my earlier attempts resembled crudely tied hair balls, the newer versions hold their shape fairly well. I owe it to learning to pack deer hair tighter (try the empty body of a ballpoint pen). John Likakis, my mentor, spins it so tightly that you can barely trim it with a single-edged razor.

Something else I discovered was how to keep my Legs from tangling by using a short, heavy leader with at least a 15-pound Maxima Chameleon tippet. I also learned to keep three or four fresh Legs on hand—dry bugs that I've previously greased with floatant. I tie it in both black and chartreuse versions, with legs to match. Lefty Kreh—who has caught practically everything that swims—suggested combining both the yellow and green shades in all my chartreuse lures. So far, it's working. As mentioned earlier, I tie the Legs weedless.

THE SNAKES ALIVE

Sometimes—especially when largemouths are celebrating their nuptials—it pays to play on their anger. They're more interested in sex than food then, but if you're willing to ignore the "do not disturb" signs, you'll get some hellacious rises from trophy-size spawners. Disturb them? That's what you're doing when you toss them this tidbit that I affectionately refer to as the Snakes Alive. It's my interpretation of a meddlesome water snake—one that appears in their honeymoon suite with larceny in mind. Snakes eat fish eggs as well as fry, and negative karma triggers angry responses, especially during the evening when snakes go a-prowlin'. See where I'm headed?

Snakes Alive

- **Hook:** #1–1/0 Tiemco 9089
- **Thread:** 10-pound Mason's hard mono or black flat waxed nylon
- **Tail/wing:** Black rabbit fur, skin colored with a black Sharpie
- **Weed guard:** 20-pound Mason's hard mono or #2 wire moustache
- **Head/body:** Black spun deer hair
- **Eyes (optional):** Large hollow plastic

Tying Tips

1. Clamp the hook securely in your vise, and bind a loop of Mason's 10-pound hard mono (or black flat waxed nylon) thread to the hook shank with the free ends pointing downward. Continue wrapping to where the hook enters the vise. When you're finished wrapping downward, bring the mono back to just ahead of the hook bend. Let the mono ends hang after grabbing them first with your hackle pliers.

2. Color the skin of a black rabbit fur strip—a fuzzy one with fairly thick skin—with a black Sharpie and set it aside to dry. The strip should measure approximately 1/4 inch in width and be 3 or 4 inches in length.

3. Tie down another loop of hard mono so that it extends approximately 3/4 inch beyond the hook. Take the strip of rabbit fur and, after trimming the hair from the first 1/2 inch of it (the hair should be pointing in the opposite direction), bind it ***hair side down*** to the hook shank at a point just above the loop butts. To make this easier to do, you may wish to taper the skin.

The Snakes Alive resembles a snake—which triggers angry responses from bedding largemouths.

4. Now you're ready to start tying down bunches of deer hair, before spinning them tightly as you work toward the hook eye. Adding a drop of tying cement (Goop diluted with toluol works for me) after each application ultimately helps strengthen the fly. Use the empty cylinder from a ballpoint pen to pack the hair bunches tightly together.
5. Remove the fly from your vise. Trim the head on the top and bottom, and then along both sides. If you shape it correctly, it should resemble a coin lying flat on its side.
6. Bring both mono ends forward, and get ready to fasten them after forcing them through the hook eye. Pull both of them backward before tying them down, making sure the loops are even. Be sure to leave plenty of clearance, so you don't interfere with the fly's hooking ability.
7. You may wish to add a pair of bubble (goo-goo) eyes, although I tend to think of it as too much trouble. Plus, if one eye gets ripped off, the fly's out of balance. If you wish to include eyes, flatten a space with your scissors and glue them in place with full-strength Goop.

I wanted this pattern to combine realism with action. And yes, I was aiming for trophy catches. The Snakes Alive pushes water like its air-breathing namesake, while displaying an accurate, menacing wriggle. That's usually enough to make a proper, bad impression.

Bass typically spawn in secluded pockets that are isolated by heavy cover—inside a circle of grass being a prime example. So when you fish this pattern, add a stout mono tippet: 15- or 20-pound test. Also, don't forget when you tie it to include a weed guard. This pattern is most effective from November to April—when big bass are bedding. Spawners prefer it 10 to 1 over my other patterns. Due to the size of the fly, and the heavier tippet, I'll toss the Snakes on a 9- or 10-weight.

Tip: Spit on your fingers and wet the wing before dressing the head with floatant. Otherwise, some dope will come off when it lands and prevent the fur from absorbing water, thereby ruining its action.

LARRY DAHLBERG'S DIVER

Dahlberg Divers feature bright saddle wings tied "outboard style," a diaphanous under collar, and the signature deer hair head. Their distinguishing feature lies just short of the diaphanous collar, where the deer hair is trimmed longer before it's coated with Goop or other thick head cement. This forms a makeshift diving plane that gives the Dahlberg Diver its signature action. The trick here is to trim a wide-enough collar, and dense-enough head, to hold its shape under repeated use. Most divers I see in fly shops feature a single mono weed guard, which, once it's bent to the side, is all but worthless.

Larry Dahlberg is an angler and tier of worldwide experience—and the recipient of numerous awards. Just this year (2017) he was inducted into the International Game Fish Association's prestigious Hall of Fame. He is also responsible for the introduction of the popular fly- and jig-tying material Flashabou.

Dahlberg Diver

- **Hook:** #1/0 Daiichi 4526
- **Thread:** Flat waxed nylon, color to match wings and body
- **Wing:** 6–8 neck hackles
- **Body:** Long flash chenille, color to match wings and collar
- **Under collar:** Marabou or rabbit that's been clipped from the skin
- **Head and collar:** Trimmed spun deer hair
- **Weed guard:** #2 wire moustache

Tying Tips

1. Fasten the hook (either a salt- or freshwater model, depending on where you intend to fish it) in your vise, and lay down a thread base at the hook bend.

2. Prepare two matched pairs of neck hackle wings—three or four feathers per side—by stripping and gluing the butts together. I prefer a single grizzly feather outside two or three solid-colored hackles per side.

Developed by Wisconsinite Larry Dahlberg, the Dahlberg Diver features a stiff hair collar that makes it dive when you twitch it and then, between twitches, bob back to the surface.

3. Measure the wings so that they're twice the length of the hook shank. Tie both halves down on top of the shank, splayed outward ("outboard style"), while pinching the butts together. The farther forward you wrap, the more pressure is applied to the thread.

4. Tie in the body and wrap your thread back to the hook bend. For the body, I want something that won't absorb water. For this and similar applications, synthetics such as Krystal Flash offer the perfect solution.

5. After taking a few half-hitches, wind your tying thread forward to just beyond the midpoint, and allow it to hang. Wind the body up to this point, and tie it down.

6. Create the collar by tying in clumps of marabou fibers or rabbit hair that's been cut from the skin. Note: I'm not a big fan of cross-cut rabbit strips—too much skin to absorb water, plus they tend to slip on the hook shank.

7. Start forming the head with a thick clump of deer hair. This time, when you pull on the thread, grip the hair in an attempt to keep it from spinning so it flares mostly on top.

8. Keep adding clumps of various colors and pushing them back, after adding a drop of cement to each set of thread wraps. When the shank is covered, take a few half-hitches and remove the fly from the vise to trim it.

9. While carefully pinching a double-edged razor blade (be careful, they're quite a bit sharper than their single-edged cousins), shape the front of the head. Then, after allowing the blade to relax, trim the bottom—and the back of the head, only now with scissors.

10. I have mentioned repeatedly my disdain for single mono weed guards, so here's what I feel is an improved replacement: a wire moustache, formed by bending a short length of #2 wire and tying it in at the nose with additional thread wraps.

Instant wobbler. A disc cut from a coffee can lid acts like a diving plane. Some tiers achieve a diving, wobbling effect by adding "lips" cut from oatmeal containers, etc., to their patterns. The action produced will be different—unless they stick to buoyant materials.

Wobble-diver. More lifelike patterns are possible with the introduction of new synthetic materials

Surface Bream Bugs

Here in Florida, the term "bream" (pronounced "brim") means sunfish—any sunfish. In fact, throughout the South, the words are synonymous. Still, when Floridians say "bream," we often, though not always, mean "bluegill."

Species aside, all bream share one thing in common: an occasional taste for floating forage, which is sure to include insects. So, at one time or another, they

Redear sunfish (aka shellcrackers) frequently rise from the depths and take surface forage.

PAT FORD PHOTO

A foam spider floats high in the film, drawing strikes from an assortment of wary panfish. I was introduced to bluegills by an old-time favorite: the Shuman's Cricket.

So many options: The author's fly box contains an assortment of bream bugs. Small floating trout flies—terrestrials, especially—are also highly effective.

rise to the surface, where fly fishers tempt them with floating "bream bugs." The simplest bugs feature tiny foam bodies and twin rubber legs. These so-called spiders ride low in the film, where they're barely visible to anglers. Like to tie one? Just lash a precut foam body—you'll find them available in fly shops, online, or in catalogs—along with a pair of rubber legs to a size 10 hook with a few turns of tying thread. Then, if you wish, add a few turns of hackle.

Me? I'm enamored with trophy bluegills. So, say you (like me) are interested in size instead of numbers. Put the odds in your favor by eliminating the small fry by upping the size of your bugs to a size 8, or sometimes a size 6, while sticking with poppers, which for reasons unknown seem to bring up more "copperheads" (large spawning bluegills). Using larger lures also decreases your chances of deep-hooking a fish that you may wish to release.

So, what's the big difference between, say, a size 8 cork popper—one that I'd use for largemouth bass—and a bona fide bream bug? None I can think of, except that most bream bugs are tied on flat rather than cup-faced bodies. Why? Because anglers fish bream bugs at rest, rather than popping and twitching them.

At least, the successful ones do. Small cork or foam bodies are the logical choice here, due to the beating they take once the fish get going.

The major difference between tying bream bugs and bass bugs is that the former require a lot less material. Both should have legs, a hackle, a tail, and, despite what you see in the stores, some sort of weed guard. As far as color, I prefer the more neutral shades. Could any of this make a difference as far as attracting, or not scaring, fish? Not always, which reminds me of a Lefty Kreh story that goes something like this:

"We'd been fishing the Rim Canal that surrounds Lake Okeechobee during a chizzywink hatch," Lefty told me. [Author's note: Chizzywinks, or blind mosquitoes—these insects don't ingest blood—are a chironomid (midge) that spends most of its life underwater, before emerging as a flying insect. The winged adults mate and then fall back to the surface, where the bluegills engulf them.] "We'd been catching an occasional bluegill until the bugs quit hatching—something that called a halt to our fishing. Meanwhile, a tree on the bank was literally white with chizzywinks that clung to its branches like snow. None, however, were hitting the surface."

What was Lefty's solution?

"We were stuck in a stalemate. So we rigged a hookless practice plug on a bait-casting outfit and cast it into the tree. All it took was a couple of yanks to get the branches moving and cause bugs by the thousands to start hitting the water."

A more elaborate cork version. Not much different from a standard cork bass bug.

The clincher?

"When the bugs started landing, the bluegills went nuts. So we picked up our fly rods and got back in the game!"

So what's the big takeaway? Forget selective feeding, or having the right shape and color, at times like these.

Speaking of bream flies, there's a time during April and May when anglers pursue huge bluegills and shellcrackers in the northwest corner of Lake Okeechobee. The lure of choice here is a black tailless weighted Woolly Worm wet fly that's tied with a grizzly hackle. The trick is to find where the fish are bedding—some old hands claim they can smell them—and toss this pattern directly onto their spawning beds. Hang on tight! These "fatties" will pop a 12-pound tippet.

Subaqueous Freshwater Patterns

Matching hatches is, at best, a crapshoot where waters run dark or murky. In Florida's Everglades, forage—everything from dragonfly nymphs and gambusia

A speckled perch (aka black crappie) gobbled this Clouser. MIKE CONNER PHOTO

It's about being prepared. I discovered plenty of wet flies in Pat Ford's freshwater fly box.

PAT FORD PHOTO

baitfish to tiny, immature bluegills and cichlids—isn't always present in sufficient numbers to alert shoreline anglers. So, unlike coldwater "emergences" with their visible feeding, predators may be picking off victims one by one, or a few at a time. So, while the object of their attention may go unnoticed, it's still important that fly fishers have the right imitation.

Even hungry fish can turn selective if their prey is available in sufficient numbers, which we, as anglers, aren't always sure of. Now, if you can't see what they're hitting, the task can be daunting. So I look for patterns that cover multiple bases—ones that take the game, so to speak, to the fish. The concept is by no means unique. Remember, the Woolly Bugger (and its variants) and the Clouser Deep Minnow—both classic multi-imitators—are "officially" wet flies or streamers. Four things that are important for a subsurface pattern are: (1) an accurate silhouette, as well as realistic movement; (2) correct size; (3) the capacity to absorb water; and (4) a medium sink rate.

WOOLLY WORMS AND BUGGERS

Woolly Worms and Buggers each define a style of tying as much as separate stand alone patterns. All have long, thin bodies wound with palmered hackles and, in the case of Buggers, long marabou tails. By varying the color or adjusting proportions—or for those willing to try it, substituting materials—tiers can achieve effects that, sometimes, enhance these patterns.

The Woolly Worm prototype, which imitates a familiar caterpillar (the woolly bear) was once popular around Lake Okeechobee, especially near Moore Haven, where monster bluegills and shellcrackers gathered in the spring to spawn. That may all be history—I haven't been back lately—but what sticks in my mind is that the time to go was during the full moon in May. More streamlined versions of their "creepy" cousins are now fished from Alaska to Patagonia, and all points in between.

I've seen Woolly Worms tied with their hackles facing forward—with bodies that float—that are designed to be fished "dry." However, the "Woolies" I'm accustomed to using call for standard chenille bodies (that, typically, I weight in the front) and soft webby hackles that break through the surface film and get down to the fish. My favorite colors are either black or chartreuse, both with grizzly hackle.

Woolly Worms—which can be tied with their hackles facing forward or backward, depending on whether you wind from the tip or the butt—have no tail or a hackle or yarn stub, whereas Buggers all have long marabou tails. With their tails—and in the Flashabugger version, sparkling bodies—Buggers imitate a wide range of forage from insects to baitfish and, in northern backwaters, leeches.

The Black Woolly, the shaggier the better, is a go-to pattern when panfish are spawning. This pattern was once much in favor around Moore Haven, Florida, on Lake Okeechobee. The locals claimed they could smell the spawning bluegill and shellcracker beds.

Marabou, we all know, is deadly wherever it's fished—especially in the presence of damsel or dragonfly nymphs. Therein, I believe, lies the key to their effectiveness. Anyone familiar with either insect knows that both their nymphs

A chartreuse Woolly Worm is a standout pattern wherever fish eat insects. While Worms have been overshadowed by their cousins the Buggers in some locations, they're the go-to fly in others.

Olive Woolly with Flashabou ribbing. I view the reason for adding lead, or a tungsten or brass bead, to flies as having less to do with their sink rate than allowing anglers to "nod" them—like a baitfish nibbling at detritus on the bottom.

are highly nutritious. I remember reading somewhere that 15 dragonfly nymphs yield approximately 100 calories—now, that's a mouthful! Judging from the number of adults in the air, it only makes sense that the nymphs must be present—hordes of them, in fact, which supports my theory.

Woolly Buggers and their variations remain my go-to patterns for fishing quiet backwaters—in both brackish and freshwater swamps—when there's no visible feeding. I'll allow one to sink near emergent vegetation before beginning a slow-twitch retrieve. Oscars and Mayans literally swarm Buggers, as do largemouth bass and all our native panfish. When I'm fishing for bedding peacocks, I keep two rods rigged: one with a purple or black Bugger, the other with a chartreuse version or variation.

In addition to being passable imitations of baitfish and insects, Buggers also excel as leech imitations. To be honest, I'm not sure how important leeches are to fish in the Everglades, but they are a major prey item in a number of stillwater habitats—especially those in colder climates where these blood-sucking flatworms attach to both warm- and cold-blooded hosts, depending on the species. They infest muddy bogs, lakes, and weed beds in slow-moving streams and rivers. No doubt, their movement—leeches swim with a slightly up-and-down, wavy motion—is an attractive motion to imitate with flies, and fish in the Everglades take leech patterns readily, fished with a more aggressive snap-strip retrieve rather than the typical leech-fisher's crawl.

Regardless of whether it imitates a minnow, insect, or leech, a purple Ultra Chenille bugger with flash running down its sides has proven its worth for both butterfly peacocks and freshwater tarpon, perhaps keying in on the darker versions, which may remind them of the ubiquitous black mollies that infest roadside canals. In fact, the darker shades—perhaps they imitate insect larvae or tiny minnows?—are more effective in our swamps than the more colorful versions. The key is to increase the durability of the pattern by reinforcing the hackle with fine gold wire or Kevlar thread.

FLASHABUGGERS

Krystal Flashabugger

- **Hook:** #6 Mustad 9672
- **Weight:** .020 or .025 lead wire, or a small brass or titanium bead
- **Thread:** Black 6/0 or 8/0, with a short length of chartreuse (optional) thread tied in to identify weighted patterns
- **Tail:** Black or olive marabou
- **Body:** Black or olive short-flash Krystal Chenille
- **Hackle:** Webby grade 2 genetic black saddle
- **Ribbing:** Black Kevlar thread or fine gold wire
- **Flash (optional):** Pearl Flashabou

Tying Tips

Tie in Kevlar thread, or fine gold wire, at the rear of the hook. After you tie in the feather in front of the fly, palmer it back to the thread or wire, then weave the thread or wire forward through the hackle, reinforcing the stem. For the tail, I use two blood plumes from which I've removed the stem tips.

Flashabugger with Mirrored Sides

Here's an even flashier version of the Krystal Flashabugger. This dressed-up Woolly Bugger, which scores points with both freshwater tarpon and butterfly peacocks, isn't far removed from less elaborate versions—except that here you add more flash and substitute Ultra Chenille for a regular chenille or cut flash body. And, if you share my preference, you keep it all purple.

- **Hook:** #6 Mustad 9672
- **Bead:** Titanium or chrome-plated brass
- **Thread:** Black Flymaster Plus
- **Tail:** 2 purple marabou plumes
- **Ribbing:** Black Kevlar thread
- **Body:** Purple Ultra Chenille
- **Flash:** Pearl Flashabou
- **Hackle:** Purple long, webby grade 2 genetic saddle

Tying Tips

1

Start out, as usual, by slipping a bead (which is easier to work with than lead wraps, and environmentally safer), small hole first, over the hook point—that's if you want the fly "nodding" between strips. Next, slide the bead all the way down to the hook eye, where you lock it in place with a series of thread wraps. Once the bead is secure, wrap your tying thread back to the hook bend, where you'll tie in the tail—typically one-and-a-half times the length of the body—along with a foot of Kevlar thread. Want the Kevlar to stay securely in place? Then tie an overhand knot near the tag end before covering where you tied it in initially with thread wraps.

2

Allow the Kevlar to hang while you wrap your tying thread forward to just behind the bead head. That's where you tie in the Ultra Chenille. After wrapping the body back to just short of the hook bend and tying it off with the Kevlar, loop two or three strands of Flashabou around the shank—so that both extend along the body—between the bead head and body. Tie them together with an overhand knot before securing them with several more thread wraps. Next, divide the Flashabou strands in half and pull them back to the hook bend, where you tie them off with the Kevlar (just like you did with the body) and then let the Kevlar dangle.

Tie in the butt of a long, webby saddle (I prefer purple) directly behind the bead head and, after taking two or three turns in place, wrap it backward toward the bend in evenly spaced spirals (typically five), overwrapping both the body and flash. Secure the hackle in place at the bend with the Kevlar. Allow the flash to extend slightly beyond the tail before tearing, rather than snipping, away the excess. Again, the trick lies in securing all the materials in place by winding the Kevlar forward in an exaggerated side-to-side motion. Make sure that the flash follows a straight line down both sides of the body by positioning it with your fingers. Over-wrap the flash, along with the hackle stem, while winding the Kevlar forward to just behind the bead head. Tie it off with your tying thread and snip off the excess, then tie your tying thread off with a series of half-hitches.

Although it's seldom fished here in Florida—or seen, for that matter—the Girdle Bug earns rave reviews from trout in the Rocky Mountain states. With its fat, juicy body and legs that flex on retrieves, it's the perfect antidote for persnickety panfish when allowed to sink and then retrieved with a snap-strip retrieve. This pattern, in hot orange, is deadly on oscars and Mayan cichlids, as well as warmouth (pictured). If you're working a bank and catching plenty of warmouths, don't expect much from largemouth bass. The two seem to be mutually exclusive. MARTY AROSTEGUI PHOTO

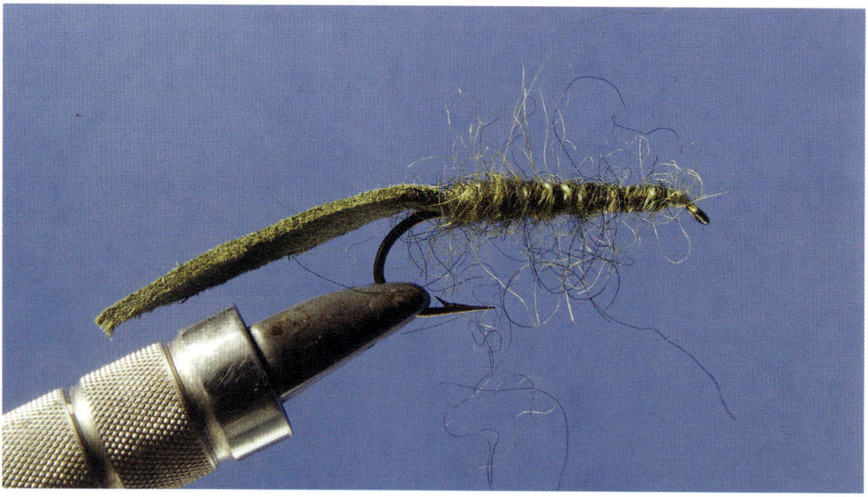

The Chamois Leech, a popular western trout fly. The tail is a thin strip of chamois, color to match body, which is wrapped with Leech Yarn. Leeches, which are common in coldwater lakes and slow-moving streams, are a major fish food.

A simple weighted marabou leech pattern. Central Florida bass expert Jon Cave reports releasing fish with their mouths covered in tiny leeches at certain times of the year.

THE SMALL STUFF

We anglers, shall we say, are *hooked* on what we once called "lunkers." Fly tiers in particular go to outrageous lengths to design outsize patterns that, we believe, big fish prefer. Granted, a few monster patterns (for example, Bob Popovics's Beast and my Legs Diamond) reap weighty rewards, but most everyday fly flingers who believe that "bigger is better" end up teetering precariously between frustration and cortisone injections.

Small Stuff

- **Hook:** #8 Mustad 9672 XL long shank
- **Bead:** Small brass
- **Thread:** Olive 8/0 Monocord
- **Weight:** Tiny brass bead
- **Tail:** 2 mottled olive turkey marabou feathers
- **Ribbing:** Cream-colored Kevlar thread
- **Body:** Medium tan Ultra Chenille
- **Hackles:** 2 turkey marabou mottled feathers

Tying Tips

1. Slide the bead, smaller hole first, onto the hook shank and push it against the hook eye. After covering the shank with olive Monocord (or a suitable substitute), take extra wraps to secure it in place.

I consider the Small Stuff my go-to "for anything small" fly. Need I say more?

2. Select two mottled olive turkey marabou feathers. Locate the stems in the tips and pluck them out with your thumb and forefinger. Tie in the plumes, butt ends forward, at the hook bend. I prefer to make the tail the same length as the hook shank. At this point, tie in a 1-foot length of cream-colored Kevlar thread and secure it by folding it and wrapping over it several times. Allow the Kevlar strand to hang.

3. At the same place you secured the other plume, tie in another marabou plume—this time by the tip (don't pick the stem), followed by a short length of tan Ultra Chenille. Wrap the tying thread forward to mid-shank, then run a fine bead of CA+ glue over the wraps (this is optional). Wind the chenille forward over the glue and tie it off. Snip off a foot-long tag of tying thread and allow it to hang from mid-shank.

4. Restart the tying thread at mid-shank and tie in a second marabou hackle and another length of chenille. Wind the thread to a point behind the head. If you wish, coat the thread wraps with CA+ before winding the chenille forward and tying it off.

5. Palmer the first marabou hackle forward (the one tied in tip first) from the tail to the midpoint. Tie it down with a whip-finish. Repeat the procedure with the second marabou hackle waiting at the midpoint, then tie it off behind the bead head. Trim any excess thread from the first wrap. Half-hitch the working thread behind the brass bead and allow your bobbin to hang.

6. Grasp the hanging Kevlar thread and wind it tightly to the head. Be careful, since Kevlar slices fingers. This overwrap protects the hackle, but be sure to wrap it with a zigzag motion to avoid crushing the marabou against the body. Tie off the Kevlar behind the head and trim. Finish the fly by whip-finishing the tying thread and trimming the Flashabou to the length of the tail. Place a drop of vinyl head cement behind the bead to secure the thread wraps.

With no apologies, I designed the Small Stuff with small fish in mind. During a typical outing, I might release a few yearling bass and/or bream, and maybe an oscar, while twitching the Small Stuff. But—depending on location—it could also be a succession of butterfly peacocks, or a smattering of snook and/or freshwater tarpon.

The Small Stuff ranks as my favorite subsurface panfish fly. Even at rest, its hackles keep breathing, while during retrieves they literally come alive. I originally designed it to fool Mayan cichlids, but it proved so successful for so many species that I decided to include it here. Officially, it's a Woolly Bugger clone, so vary your retrieves to imitate baitfish, crustaceans, or nymphs. So, what's the big difference between this and more standard Bugger versions? Mottled turkey marabou feathers tied in series. Remember, here it's all about extra action and color—and size.

Tiny tarpon, although sometimes present in incredible numbers, require the right presentation and correct fly pattern where fresh and salt waters meet.

The Salt Marsh

Tucked away along Florida's southern periphery lies a landscape of unimaginable beauty—if your taste leans toward hardscrabble hammocks or endless vistas of mangroves and saw grass. It's where marshes, and the trees that grow between them, surround otherwise unremarkable waterways—unremarkable, unless you're a predator.

No one knows this area better than J. M. "Chico" Fernandez, who's been fishing these waters since the early 1960s. Fernandez arrived here from Cuba by ferry—he still refers to himself as the "Original Cuban Fly Fisherman" (having previously caught snook, bass, and bonefish on his native island)—in 1959, along with his mother and a blue 190SL Mercedes. The car figures prominently in Chico's affair with this region. "Brackish water [which you'll typically find here] flows through my veins," he tells me. "More than bonefish—or even billfish—I love chasing snook and tarpon across this varied landscape, either

Skip Clement of Flylifemagazine.com hoists a salt marsh snook. Fish this size and larger are standard fare amid the mangroves.

***Left:** Chico Fernandez unhooks an obstreperous "puppy drum," or juvenile redfish. Less temperature-sensitive than either snook or tarpon, some redfish remain in the marsh until late in the fall.* ***Right:** Salt marsh pioneer Chico Fernandez displays a small tarpon. Chico, who's been fishing the Tamiami Trail since the 1960s, says the canal has narrowed from when he first fished it, due to siltation.* CHICO FERNANDEZ PHOTOS

by canoe or on foot. Here, you become a part of nature—up close and personal. Most gamefish in these canals feed on the tiniest of baitfish, calling for exact imitation and accurate casts."

Chico initially fished with a handful of like-minded anglers: "Little John" Emery, Flip Pallot, Bill Curtis, Norm Duncan—guys he met at the Tackle Box, then a popular Miami fly shop. When they first got together, no one had boats, but they all had heard the rumors: There were fish to be had in the newly dug canals of southwestern Florida! The results of this fusion became salt marsh traditions.

Bill—the oldest of the group and, at the time, a professional photographer—had a friend named Rocky Weinstein. A salt marsh regular, as well as the prototypical land captain (sound familiar?), Weinstein would meet his clients near Chokoloskee, after which he'd search the canals for snook and tarpon. He drove an old Studebaker that he'd stuffed with fly rods that he fashioned from 7½-foot spin blanks—which he hoped to sell. Outdoor writer Charley Waterman—whom I had the pleasure of knowing and fishing with—was another Weinstein crony. According to Charley, Rocky fell into the "land-guiding" habit due to his inability

Reel designer Ted Juracsik waits for a truck to pass before casting. These roadside canals host snook, tarpon, and redfish—along with freshwater species.

to read nautical charts. Remember, where he fished was next door to the inscrutable Ten Thousand Islands.

After Weinstein's charters ended, and if snook had been hitting, he'd ring up Curtis, who lived in Miami. Then Curtis and Chico would hop in Chico's Mercedes and race off toward the marsh at breakneck speed. It was a marriage made in heaven.

So, what patterns did these guys use when they got there?

"In the beginning, it was mostly small Muddlers. Then, as we learned more, we shifted to sliders," said Chico. "We also used feather-winged streamers, especially a white, yellow, and grizzly version of the Sea-Ducer that we referred to as a 'Shrimp,' and small, layered-wing bucktails that we tied with black over brown over white." (The Sea-Ducer, allegedly introduced by former game warden Homer Rhode, is also known as the Homer Rhode Streamer.)

Those were days of discovery, when a group of young anglers forged fly-fishing history. The salt marsh was—and still is—a daunting and unfamiliar venue, where the slightest nuance could make or break the fishing. As Chico put it: "We'd sand our [rod] blanks in order to change the action, make our own guides—stuff like that. We didn't have much to go on, so we made our own rules." And now 60 years later, those rules and the same fly patterns—along with a few new ones—still apply.

The yellow Marabou Muddler is a strong contender for "Fly of the Year" wherever fresh and salt waters meet. Blame it all on visibility and action.

Homer Rhode's Shrimp Fly—aka Sea-Ducer—is an early southwest Florida pattern that remains effective. The wing can be tied either "inboard" or "outboard" with more hackles, if desired.

What makes the salt marsh so different from other South Florida venues? How about the profound abundance of micro-forage, plus the unusual number of outsize predators—from both salt and fresh water—that scale down their appetites when they enter the salt marsh? The result requires precise imitation on the part of anglers.

One of the author's salt marsh fly boxes. Note the Rivets for snook and Black Death streamers for tarpon.

Here, bigger is seldom better: tiny flies that score in the salt marsh.

A typical pusher-style fly that excels in the salt marsh. Did I hear someone mention spun deer hair? MIKE CONNER PHOTO

Lefty Kreh displaying what today may seem unbelievable: limits of giant bass caught just east of the salt marsh. BERNARD "LEFTY" KREH PHOTO

Fish here feed primarily on strong falling tides, when the water turns murky. This, in turn, puts a premium on locating forage. Watch any of the region's more common baitfish—gambusias, mollies, pike killifish—and you'll discover that all have one thing in common: a similar style of locomotion, swimming across the surface while pushing a head wake. Therein, I believe, lies the key to explosive fishing. All successful salt marsh patterns move water, whether as the result of deer hair or fur heads or tightly bunched hackles.

The conundrum works both ways. When Lefty Kreh ran the Metropolitan

Tiny pike killifish is an invasive species that brings out the aggression in large salt marsh snook. PHOTO COURTESY OF USGS

Miami Fishing Tournament (aka the Miami MET), for years the world's largest free fishing tournament, he'd fish the eastern edge of the marsh where the water remained perpetually fresh—using flies by day and plug gear by night. What he did was strictly bass fishing. We spoke often of this incredible resource—one that, at the time, appeared inexhaustible. Yet, while things aren't what they used to be, the rules remain constant.

When bass reside in a true freshwater habitat, they feed on the full-size forage that you'd expect to find there—say, frogs or juvenile bluegills—but once they move into the salt marsh, they start feeding selectively on tiny baitfish. The same holds true for snook (or tarpon) in saltwater rivers, once they move inland into brackish water. That's not to say there aren't exceptions. But for the most part, fish in the salt marsh insist on tiny flies—typically waking patterns—that show up well against the discolored background.

Sunken Salt Marsh Patterns

In a place where predators feed almost exclusively on baitfish, effective fly patterns are by nature subsurface—with a few exceptions—but just how far down is another matter. If there's a cardinal rule in this swampy morass, it's to stick with patterns that move lots of water—and, in most cases, make surface impressions, either with deer or craft hair heads or thick hackle collars.

If I had to pick just a few subsurface favorites, I'd include the following:

Glades Minnow: Mike Conner's original, and still just as effective wherever big fish are feeding on tiny gambusias and mollies. I prefer Glades Minnows tied in sizes 4 and 6, with a few size 8s thrown in for good measure. Thanks to a chance discovery, I now tempt these "monsters" with very small flies.

Suescun's Conehead: Perhaps the best all-around fly in the entire mangrove backcountry. Fish it "dry," and it chugs on the surface like a typical greased hair bug. But trim the head smaller and soak it with head cement, and you end up with a pattern that moves just beneath the surface—and still pushes water.

Rivet, improved version: Similar, but easier to tie than the Conehead and nearly as effective—especially for tarpon. Once again, I keep the deer hair head small in order to fish this pattern beneath the surface.

Squid Fly: Another highly effective deer hair pattern. I've heard it said that roadside tarpon here will only hit two patterns: black ones and white ones. Well, here's my pick of the latter. My abbreviated version of Lou Tabory's proven design is just the ticket when the light is right and the fish are selective. Note: It makes sense to carry both light and dark versions of any pattern—although with this one I don't.

Schminnow: These are my go-to choices whenever fish are showing and there's no visible surface feeding. Rolling tarpon in deep water is but one example.

Small group of subsurface oddballs: Patterns that address the occasional, off-beat need. Take tiny shrimp flies for days when the snook are feeding exclusively on grass shrimp, or any number of tiny wet flies if you're into battling oscars and Mayan cichlids. Here, the Small Stuff comes highly recommended.

Glass minnow–style pattern: You'll find plenty to choose from—for those times when you're imitating thin, tiny "rain bait." While I steer clear of skinny patterns that slip through the water without a commotion, I recognize their place here—as well as anywhere else predators target tiny, slim baitfish.

"Expanded" hair and synthetic pattern that imitates tiny bluegills and cichlids: A relatively new concept that keeps proving itself. As cichlid populations in the salt marsh canals keep expanding, the predators' habits are changing. Specifically, they're adjusting their menus. Based on the occasional selective feeding I've seen on small Mayan cichlids—mostly by snook—I now carry flies that address this situation.

MIKE CONNER'S GLADES MINNOW

When it was first introduced nearly 30 years ago, the Glades Minnow was hailed as the quintessential Everglades fly. Created by Stuart, Florida, angler, guide, freelance columnist, and environmentalist Mike Conner while attempting to imitate the tiny molly and gambusia (mosquito fish) baitfish found in salt marsh creeks and roadside ditches, the Glades Minnow is now a backwater staple.

Glades Minnow

- **Hook:** #2–4 Mustad 34007
- **Thread:** Mono, to match wing
- **Wing:** White, tan, and olive Craft Fur
- **Body:** Gold or copper spooled tinsel
- **Ribbing:** X-small V-Rib or similar
- **Eyes:** X-small red/black or yellow/black decal eyes

Tying Tips

Since it's tied completely from synthetics, keeping this pattern riding upright presents a problem. However, if the leader's not overly heavy, and if it's been straightened, the fly's epoxied eyes add enough weight to serve as a makeshift "keel." Proportion is all-important. When viewed from the side, the fly's blocky silhouette should resemble any baitfish that captured snook and tarpon have managed to regurgitate.

If necessary, I taper the Craft Fur with scissors and trim the Flashabou by breaking it off between my thumb and forefinger. This creates a frazzled effect that adds realism.

Mike Conner's classic Glades Minnow. This fly proves highly effective for salt marsh species. For anyone interested in an accurate imitation of "hardhead" baitfish, this fly remains the pattern of choice.

As a matter of choice, Mike occasionally fits his flies with moustache weed guards—which grants him access to the snag-filled haunts where snook frequently feed. Tie one in at the head, using a piece of 10-pound Mason's hard mono.

Glades Minnow (Kantner Variation)

- **Hook:** #6 or 4 Mustad 34007
- **Thread:** Clear fine monofilament
- **Body:** Fine gold Mylar braid wrapped over rear half of the shank
- **Wing:** Green over yellow chartreuse, striped with permanent marker
- **Flash:** Gold Angel Hair or substitute
- **Head:** Clumps of combed-out acrylate green chartreuse fuzz, tied wool-head style and trimmed
- **Eyes:** Reflective gold or red decal

Mike tied his original version to tempt snook and tarpon in the Tamiami Trail canal. Since then, the Glades Minnow has proven its effectiveness for a variety of species—wherever and whenever it's fished—not to mention that it's one of the earliest examples of the use of Craft Fur in saltwater tying. According to Mike, he designed his Glades Minnow, trademarked as Conner's Glades Minnow by Umpqua Feather Merchants, and marketed as such, as "a 'match-the-hatch pattern' for fish such as snook, baby tarpon, largemouth bass, and other species that are single-mindedly feeding on gambusia baitfish (so-called mosquito minnows) that are a common forage in estuarine waters. It is a deadly fly for that application, but not as effective as a 'search pattern' when fish are not visibly feeding." After casting to the opposite bank, Mike allows his fly to sink for several seconds before beginning a short, jerky retrieve. The strike usually comes within a few feet of its onset.

The defining feature of this subsurface pattern is its expanded "underfur" head. Savvy backwater anglers recognize the ability to move water as the trigger whenever they're mimicking "hardheads." To create this effect, Mike used a comb to collect the acrylate fuzz from Craft Fur backing before tying it in small clumps at a time—in the manner of a "wool head." However, unlike wool, Craft Fur sheds water, making the Glades Minnow lighter and easier to cast. If it's tied correctly, you won't see the tying thread. This seamless effect results from a careful melding of body and wing materials, the monofilament thread, and head cement. Although Mike created his pattern to imitate brackish baitfish, it can be used to represent other blunt-nosed species. And since the Glades Minnow

My chartreuse and gold version of the Glades Minnow proves highly effective for summer tarpon in off-color water. This fly stands out like a stop sign. Since the Glades Minnow is constructed entirely from synthetics, it's advisable to substitute a drop of superglue for head cement after each of the tying steps. For durability, place a drop of 5-minute epoxy over each eye after attaching.

represents a style of tying, not just a stand-alone recipe, it can be tied in bright colors and fished as an attractor.

I usually prefer Glades Minnows tied in neutral shades—typically light and dark browns with gold bodies and flash—on size 4 and 6 hooks, although in apparent contradiction, I'll sometimes reach for a yellow/green-chartreuse version that's a "killer" for backcountry tarpon under low-light conditions. Most Everglades baitfish are measured in millimeters, making accurate imitations a bit tricky to fish. But "guppies" and mollies occasionally grow larger—to size 2 or even a 1. And that, my friends, is a meal. Larger Glades Minnows are also deadly on those rare occasions you locate big sailfin mollies.

While fishing this pattern together, Mike and I have taken hundreds of snook from areas most anglers ignore. The Glades Minnow helped jump-start my backcountry career, before I discovered the Conehead and Squid Fly—or developed the Rivet. It also travels extremely well. In a totally irrelevant aside, I caught one of the largest rainbow trout of my angling career on a size 6 Glades Minnow—which I tied to match the forage in the lake I was fishing. The original Glades Minnow remains my go-to pattern wherever well-fed snook demand tiny, exact imitations.

Nymphing the Minnow

I'm reminded of a day early on in my guiding, when I hooked several dozen snook in quick succession, and lost most of them to tackle failures. All, I believe, weighed at least 8 pounds; a few looked better than 20. But since they were feeding on "rain bait," my choice of flies was a size 6 Glades Minnow, which I tied directly to my 12-pound-test tippet. This all took place within a few yards of a major highway. I can still close my eyes and hear traffic whizzing past me, while I kept casting to full-blown splashes. The melee—true mayhem for as long as it lasted—centered around a single run-out. But try as I might, I couldn't buy a strike as I covered the outlet.

I saw breaking fish wherever I looked, and I cast repeatedly in an effort to trick one. Yet none would oblige until I stumbled upon a technique that a freshwater trout fisherman would have tried a lot earlier: fishing the fly like a dead-drifted nymph.

I'd been casting to swirls and foamy concussions, while trying different retrieves, when I paused to brush off a bug. That's when the first snook hit. Although the hook pulled free a few seconds later, the same thing happened on a subsequent cast—once again, when I stopped my retrieve. When I paused to reflect, it all made sense. No matter how lifelike my fly appeared, these snook weren't interested in single inch-long baitfish. They wanted a mouthful instead, something they achieved by rushing the schools, then circling back and inhaling the cripples. Had I discovered the secret? Were they gulping micro-forage like glutted whales, with mouths agape in a sea full of krill?

What if I allowed my fly to sink, without imparting any movement? I'd watch the line point; if and when it twitched, I'd strike. I could barely believe what happened next. After dropping my fly where snook had been splashing, I gave it time to sink, but a snook inhaled it before it ever reached bottom, heralding a succession of identical responses. Now, whenever my line twitched, I'd raise my rod into a bragging-size fish—that took off down the ditch with me in hot pursuit. I spent the next two hours dodging cattails, instead of casting in vain and tearing my hair out.

By the time the tide finally turned, I'd beached two or three nice ones, after parting company with countless others. Either the hook would pull out, due to the narrow gape, or the fish eventually frayed through my 12-pound tippet. It was maddening, I admit, but a thrill ride, too. Now all I needed was a pattern that I could tie on a larger hook. Larger Glades Minnows opened to mixed reviews, so I kept on experimenting with details: new styles of tying, different retrieves. Supersize Glades Minnows seemed to work okay, but only in the presence of larger forage—just what you'd expect from exact imitations. The nymphing technique, however, was really the "keeper." ■

ALEX SUESCUN'S CONEHEAD

When it comes to waylaying snook, veteran anglers rely on time-tested hard baits—because they've proven so effective. That's what Alex Suescun had in mind when he created his iconic Conehead streamer. Like its inspiration, the Creek Chub Darter, his version swims with a pronounced side-to-side motion that drives predators wild. By combining soft wings and a diaphanous collar, and adding a specially trimmed head, Suescun created a combined imitator/attractor that's effective wherever you fish—not just in the salt marsh.

Conehead

- **Hook:** #4-1/0 Mustad 34007
- **Thread:** Flat waxed nylon
- **Wing:** 2 preassembled hackle halves, each consisting of 3–5 saddles, the outermost of which are grizzlies
- **Flash:** Pearl Flashabou
- **Collar:** Marabou or rabbit fur that's been cut from the hide
- **Head:** Spun deer hair that's been carefully tapered and sliced with a razor

The signature deer hair head gave the Conehead its name, along with its action. This one was tied by Jody Moore. According to Moore, "It works equally well in salt water or brackish. It's particularly effective under low-light conditions, or whenever the wind dies and the surface glasses over." JODY MOORE PHOTO

Tying Tips

1. Start out by gluing the wing butts together. In order to perfectly match the hackles, select four solid-colored saddles of similar shape and curvature before measuring the stems. Since I prefer to make Conehead wings equal to two-and-a-half times the shank length, I have a premeasured cardboard "template." After lining up the hackle tips at one mark, I use my scissors point to score the barbs. Incidentally, if you intend to make hackle wings on a regular basis, now's the time to measure additional marks for other hook sizes.

After scoring the hackles, strip away the excess barbs with your thumb and fingernail before trimming the stems. Touch the butts with a drop of Flexament before fitting the two sections together and setting them aside to dry.

2. Select two grizzly saddles approximately two-thirds the length of the glued solid-color "halves." Peel away any excess fibers and paste the grizzly feathers to the outside curve of the wing sections with another drop of Flexament before allowing the completed sections to dry.

3. Lock the hook in your vise and cover the shank to the halfway point with flat waxed nylon, then bring the thread back to the bend. If you plan on using a wing separator, tie it in now, making sure to keep it shorter than the hackle wings.

4. While positioning each completed wing segment on top of the shank (but outside the separator), tie them in. If the feathers have a slight curve, I tie them "inboard" style, although with rooster saddles, there's not much curvature. Incidentally, it helps to leave the hackle butts exposed before adding flash. Some anglers prefer to create additional bulk by tying in an overwing of bucktail or other hair. If you do, allow it to extend slightly beyond the hackles in order to create a tapered silhouette.

5. If you wish to add flash, hold a few strands of pearl Flashabou by both ends and hook the midpoint over the exposed hackle butts. Pull both ends backward along the center line while binding them down with tying thread. Don't wrap too far back or you'll twist the wing. Then, after touching the wraps with a drop of Flexament, bring the thread forward to a point at the front of the wing wraps.

6. A soft collar separates the wing and deer hair head. Some tiers tie in cross-cut rabbit and wind it forward (after gluing over the thread wraps); I prefer to use hair snipped from the hide or marabou tufts. In order to make a usable tuft, I first pluck the stems from the end of a "blood" plume before bunching the tips and snipping the feather. Occasionally, if the marabou's dense enough, you can use fibers from the side of the quill.

The collar should be half the length of the wing when tied in at the front of the wing-wraps. Keep in mind that marabou is easier to work with when it's wet. Normally, three plumes will do the job (one each for the top of the fly and the sides), but you're lucky if you get a good plume from each feather.

7. Select a piece of tough, compactable deer hair. Start by spinning a deer collar and continue adding hair, while twisting and pushing each bundle tightly to the rear with a "pusher." Be sure to add a drop of Flexament between each application. My two favorite versions of this fly feature a chartreuse or red nose, so I spin dyed hair in my final two applications. When you're finished adding deer hair, tie a whip-finish in the thread.

8. Now's when you shape and trim the head. First, remove the fly from the vise. What I try to do next is create the triangular shape responsible for the Conehead's action. If you trim the head properly, it will ultimately display three edges sharp enough to cut through the water (like a plug). Proper clipping takes practice, so don't despair. Keep in mind that even if you're too ambitious, you'll still have a "hackle Muddler."

If the hair's been properly packed, it should be evenly flared. Begin shaping the head by trimming the bottom flat along the hook shank. Remember that getting close is important for balance as well as clearance, so elevate the hackles with your fingers in order to avoid cutting the wing.

After trimming the bottom, angle your scissors backward along the head in order to make a diagonal cut. Keep the blades on a bias, with the finger holes near the nose and the points extending back and outside of the wing to get the proper angle. Make a single cut, keeping the top blade in position along the "crown" of the head. Retrace this cut from the back, snipping forward, then lay your scissors along the opposite side of the head and repeat the procedure. These cuts should create sharp edges along the sides of the deer hair. Examine the fly from the front. At this point, you should clearly see the signature triangle shape. After trimming with the scissors, fine-tune the head with a disposable razor.

9. As a final touch, coat the head with Flexament. Allow the fly to dry before adding optional solid plastic or decal eyes.

The result of shaving the tightly packed head? A pattern that literally "cuts" through the water, while displaying the unbeatable bounce that the hackles and collar offer. Watch a Conehead in action and you'll see it: a visual that's seldom lost on the fish. The hollow hair head, which is naturally buoyant, lets you fish this fly as a waking pattern. Or, depending on how you trim it—and whether or not you grease or coat it with head cement—the Conehead can be twitched as a slider or retrieved just under the surface.

The first one I saw had an oversize head and heavily dressed wings, but the dressing can be modified to suit an angler's specific requirements. My salt marsh friends like theirs tied in white, black, or yellow—with grizzly outer wings—and they fish them mostly as splashy attractors. But they also fish neutral versions that I now believe imitate a sought-after baitfish. Although I've always felt that

In 1951 Harold LeMaster and Phil Shriner joined forces in Clearwater, Florida, and founded the L & S Bait Company. The company's signature product—a plug with reflective sides—was (and still is) known as the L & S MirrOlure. MirrOlures are deadly on snook. One particular model, the 52M11 (red/white head, with silver sides), was such a standout that it was eventually copied by fly tiers. In some ways the MirrOlure Fly resembles a Conehead; however, this one's narrower tapered head gives it less radical action. TIED BY ROAN ZUMFELDE

the Conehead resembled nothing in particular, it looks enough like a pike killifish to make me question my judgment. Pike killifish grow considerably larger than guppies or mollies, so the hook, for a change, needn't be so tiny. I suggest you also tie up a few in brighter colors (for example, chartreuse and pink) for use in murky water, but in general outlandish colors or excessive flash don't produce as well as more subdued versions.

The Conehead excels whenever predators aren't keying on anything special. Since, technically speaking, these flies are "attractors," I don't worry as much about matching sizes (à la the Glades Minnow), so I tie them on larger hooks. It's one of the few examples in the salt marsh where bigger is better, although I seldom resort to anything larger than a size 1.

On the subject of hook size, tarpon, our largest backwater gamefish, prefer size 4s or 6s in most of the patterns we use here. However, with that small a fly, you're stuck using lighter tippets, so the fish fray through them or the hook tears out after a protracted battle. Use anything larger and they ignore it—but not so with Coneheads.

A few years back, I discovered a veritable Shangri-la: a lagoon awash with rolling tarpon. They remained where I'd found them for several weeks running, despite the proximity of passing traffic. Apparently, nobody saw them. Whatever the reason, this place was made to order. When I first encountered them, they appeared to be totally listless, confining their movements to infrequent forays down a distant line of mangroves, where they fed half-heartedly on nondescript forage—hardly what I'd call an adrenaline rush. I wondered if I could tempt even one to hit, let alone enjoy spectacular fishing. That brings up a point: Whatever feeding I saw lacked the least conviction, yet I knew these tarpon had to be burning calories. I was anxious to try them, but in order to do so, I needed a strategy.

So one day I launched my canoe through a mangrove tangle, in an attempt at concealment. Then, I sculled on my hands and knees across the channel before noiselessly poling into position. Finally, I drove my push pole into a shallow sandbar, where I could cover the tarpon from several angles. Could I meet the challenge? Well, I discovered several of their idiosyncrasies right off the bat, like how they were quick to spook from the slightest shadow, or how they'd vanish completely if they suspected my presence.

When I showed them a fly, the laid-up fish—the spookiest of all—remained oblivious, while the ones in the current simply quit rolling. My fingers trembled each time I changed flies. But regardless of the pattern, the fish failed to respond. I never got so much as a flash. That's until I noticed a Conehead—tied on a whim, thinking someday I'd try it—under a roll of leader that I'd stashed in my fly box. I figured "Why not?" No sooner had the Conehead landed than it vanished abruptly in a washtub-size swirl. I was dumbstruck, to say the least. The fish threw the fly on the second jump.

That particular fly was an abbreviated version, tied with a lacquered head. But regardless of its fine points, the fish attacked it. After hooking six in a row, and releasing a 20-pounder, I clipped off the Conehead and headed for shore. Then, when I got home, I tied several more. I tried other patterns over the next few weeks. While the occasional fish showed a token interest, nothing came close to matching the Conehead. It was like throwing a roast beef sandwich to a Labrador retriever.

Though it takes a little longer to tie than some patterns, the Conehead remains one of my all-time favorites for backwater tarpon. I used one to catch (and release) my largest creek tarpon, an approximate 60-pounder. Snook like it, too, especially the big fall-run fish that swim up from the Gulf. They're accustomed to larger fare for a change, so I don't waste time with tiny offerings—one of the few times when bigger is better (well, not too big). Instead, I rely on white, pink, or chartreuse Coneheads (depending on water clarity) tied on a size 1 hook.

THE RIVET

My earlier attempts in the backcountry had proved futile. Where to start, I wondered, as far as imitating forage or fishing attractor patterns? Then, what type of forage should I try to imitate? Although I saw visible feeding, I seldom got strikes. I'd already begun experimenting with exact imitations, and had recently discovered Suescun's Conehead. But each had its drawbacks. Snook frequently ignored the flamboyant Conehead, especially when feeding on tiny "rain bait." Then, when I imitated the latter with a tiny Connor's Glades Minnow, the fish might not hit it—or if they did, the hook sometimes pulled out after a lengthy battle. I needed an offer they couldn't refuse in a size that suited my purpose.

Rivet (Improved)

- **Hook:** #2–4 Mustad 34007
- **Thread:** White flat waxed nylon or Monocord
- **Wing:** Light brown and tan Craft Fur
- **Flash:** Pearl Angel Hair
- **Collar:** Natural and white rabbit fur
- **Head:** Spun and trimmed gray deer or elk hair

Whimsically, the Rivet resembles its namesake, which join the strips of siding that line these highways. While the Rivet, in some ways, resembles a Conehead—at least, to the untrained eye—the similarity ends in the hackle or Craft Fur wings (depending on which version), a diaphanous collar, and a deer hair head. The Rivet was always my go-to pattern when fishing the salt marsh, where I did most of my guiding.

Tying Tips

1. Clamp a de-barbed (the fly will last longer, and catch just as many fish) hook in the vise.

2. Tie in the Craft Fur wing just ahead of the hook bend. Colors are optional, but I prefer light brown layered over tan. The wing should measure twice the length of the hook shank. Afterward, coat the thread wraps with head cement and allow to dry.

3. Remove the fly from the vise. Add three black vertical stripes to the synthetic wing with a fine-point Sharpie marking pen. When the ink dries, return the fly to the vise

4. Add a few strands of pearl Angel Hair alongside the wing, then tear, rather than snip off, the excess. This allows a hint of flash to trail behind the wing during retrieves. Again, coat the thread wraps with head cement, and allow to dry.

5. When the glue dries, create a collar by snipping a pinch of white rabbit fur from the skin before tying it in. Coat the thread wraps, then add a second collar of gray-brown, well-marked rabbit that's two-thirds the length of the white one. Incidentally, I prefer snipped hair over cross-cuts, insofar as there's no skin to slip or absorb water. When tying in the collar, measure so it's approximately half the length of the wing.

6. Once again, coat the thread wraps with head cement. Then, with the glue partly dry, spin a tight head of gray deer or elk hair and tie off the thread.

7. Remove the fly from the vise and trim the head to a small conical shape.

Rivet (Original)

- **Hook:** #4 Mustad 34007
- **Thread:** Gray Monocord
- **Tail/wing:** Grizzly neck hackles tied "inboard" style, or barred Craft Fur layered brown over tan
- **Flash:** Silver Angel Hair
- **Two-part collar:** Natural brown rabbit fur over slightly longer white rabbit fur "skirt"
- **Head:** Tapered gray deer hair

I needed a pattern that combines the best of both worlds, and the Rivet was it. In addition to displaying accurate coloration (or better, the lack of it), along with translucence, this pattern's side-to-side wobble brought the snook a-runnin'. Whereas the Rivet's wobble is less than that of the Conehead due to the substitution of a stiffer hackle or Craft Fur wing, it derives sex appeal from its heavily dressed collar—actually two collars in one. I know of no other streamer that can make that claim. Plus, I could also tie it in larger sizes and still get plenty of hits. I didn't realize why at the time.

Completed Rivet with trimmed deer hair head. The double-skirted collar allows a hint of white to show beneath the natural rabbit.

Admittedly, the Conehead and Glades Minnow helped get me get my start, but the Rivet put me in business. The Rivet introduced me to unprecedented numbers of snook, my go-to salt marsh species. Displacement is king in the salt marsh. Since you're frequently fishing in off-color water, flies that create shock waves draw the attention. With the Rivet, however, it's mostly the two-part collar (imagine a lady's skirt and the slip beneath it) that pulses and bounces during snap-strip retrieves. In addition to performing as an attractor fly, the Rivet imitates an extremely desirable nonnative baitfish: the vaunted pike killifish.

If you're unfamiliar with this bite-size tidbit—it reaches 6 inches or more in length—you're not alone. Pike killifish resemble baby "northerns" (pike), yet they're the pièce de résistance of salt marsh forage. Snook love them so much that, if they discover even a few, they forget about "rain bait" and go for the gusto. Pike killifish invariably swim on the surface, where between short bursts, they curl their tails like a seahorse. It's this run-and-curl signature that predators look for. I've watched snook chase killies to where it literally resembled sailfish showering ballyhoo. Then, wherever the killies landed, more snook were waiting. My customers and I interviewed countless victims, and one thing we're sure of: If the water's off-color and killifish are present, it's time to haul out a Rivet.

Other reasons that make this pattern a winner? Its sturdy, easy-to-tie construction makes the Rivet an ideal choice for demanding conditions: say, constant guiding in the mangrove morass, where the shelf life of flies is measured in minutes. Snook and tarpon definitely prefer my improved version with synthetics to the original Rivet tied with all-natural materials. Plus, the use of synthetics shortens the tying process, which if you're forced to tie flies for a living, makes life a lot simpler. For best results, I retrieve the Rivet in short, snappy strips with distinct pauses between them.

LOU TABORY'S SQUID FLY

Designed by Northeastern surf guru Lou Tabory, the Squid Fly lives up to its name. On fast-strip retrieves, the herl comes alive, causing the fly to resemble its namesake. But you won't find squid in the swamps or salt marsh, so it must be this fly's overall sex appeal—call it bounce or flourish—that salt marsh predators can't resist. This, when combined with its ease of tying, ranks the Squid Fly among my all-time favorites.

I first saw this fly in a book or a magazine, possibly Lefty Kreh's *Saltwater Fly Patterns*. The deer hair head must have caught my eye—after all my carping about "displacement." What I eventually did, however, was take someone else's pattern and gently buff it in order to suit my needs: specifically, imitating gambusia baitfish. While the monster stripers that Tabory beaches would sneeze at my miniscule fly speck, backcountry predators view their menus from a different perspective. But you already know that, having read this far in the salt marsh chapter.

There's a saying in the salt marsh that tarpon in the roadside canals hit only two patterns: black ones and white ones. Try as I might, I haven't been able to debunk it. As far as a white one, the Squid Fly is a major contender, and of all the backwater tarpon flies I deal with, it's one of the easiest to tie.

Squid Fly (Kantner version)

- **Hook:** #2–4 Mustad 34007
- **Thread:** White flat waxed nylon
- **Wing:** 15–20 white ostrich herls, clipped from near the tip of the quill
- **Collar:** Several tufts of white rabbit fur, clipped from a skin
- **Head:** Spun white and chartreuse deer hair

Tying Tips

1. Clamp the hook in your vise and lay down a base of tying thread, starting at the halfway point on the hook shank and working backward to the hook bend.

2. Select a white ostrich plume and snip 15 to 20 herls from the quill. You'll find the best ones near the tip; however, the others can be substituted without much loss of action. In my line of work, you learn to make do.

3. Arrange the herls with their tips together and then spit on your fingertips to wet them. Take this makeshift "wing" and tie it down just ahead of the hook bend. I sometimes grab a few strands of a flexible Mylar flash material (such as Angel Hair) and catch the midpoint over the wing butts before drawing the ends backward along both sides and tying them in on top of the herls.

4. Bring your thread forward and then snip a pencil-size chunk of white rabbit fur from a processed skin. I've never liked the cross-cut strips; they tend to slip and the skin absorbs water. Tie the hair down just ahead of the wing butts. This "skirt" should measure approximately one-third the length of the wing fibers. Touch a drop of thinned head cement (I prefer Goop and toluol) to the thread wraps and allow it to sink into the wing butts.

5. Add additional rabbit fur if necessary, keeping in mind that more may be better. When this step is completed, you should still have ½ inch of bare hook shank remaining on which to spin a deer hair head.

6. Create a deer hair head by adding small pinches of white body hair and locking them in place after allowing the hair to spin. Pack the hair tightly with your fingers (better yet, with the tip section of a ballpoint pen). Follow each application with a drop of head cement. Meanwhile, keep in mind that the secret to tight, neatly formed heads is mostly a matter of selecting quality materials—or, in the case of deer hair, those of the right consistency (short and hollow, but not too soft). Finish off the head with a pinch of chartreuse hair before removing the fly from the vise and trimming the head to size.

Most of what I did here was tinker with proportions, while adjusting the size of the fly to that of the local forage. There are, however, a few minor changes. Take, for example, the bicolor head: You can take my word for it that chartreuse

This snook shows off a Squid Fly—a miniature version of Lou Tabory's classic striper pattern.

attracts tarpon, although I still can't remember why I decided to try it. Work this fly with distinct twitches and pauses between them. I don't use so much hair that the fly won't sink—preferring instead a "waking" pattern. This one draws strikes when the fish are beneath bridges, but especially when they're tootling in and out of the mangroves. It's not unusual to get several hits on a single cast, so keep stripping until you hook a fish.

ESTAZ MINNOW AND SCHMINNOW

On those blistering days when the breeze dies and the surface slicks over, driving down dissolved oxygen levels even further, the fish shift into neutral. But it's also when splashy behavior erupts in the deeper lakes and channels, along with occasional outbursts of what looks like shoreline feeding—with the accent on "occasional." At these times, although the fish may refuse other popular patterns, they'll sometimes react to a Woolly Bugger—or one of its clones. Various Bugger variations can be just the ticket for tarpon due to their flash and seductive action that can be seen even deep in the water column—sometimes, that is.

I remember guiding an editor/publisher of a saltwater fly magazine. I was paddling my canoe on just such an occasion, when he released two small tarpon.

Buggers and their clone, the Estaz Minnow. Estaz Minnows are both effective and easy to tie.

He pulled this off while nothing was visibly feeding—by twitching a Bugger. While I don't count this as stellar fishing, it saved the day for an aspiring writer (and guide). But that's not the first—nor the last—time something similar happened, mostly on backwater tarns like the one I described.

The Estaz Minnow and its alter ego, the Schminnow, display many of the good points of a properly tied Flashabugger. Plus—here's the best part—they take less

Roan zumFelde of Naples, Florida, ties an effective version of the Woolly Bugger. Roan's been fishing the salt marsh since before I met him. Along with Captain Jim Grace and the late Pete Villani, he's put the "Gulf Coast spin" on flies that I frequently find myself tying and using.

time to tie. Both are excellent go-to patterns whenever you're faced with fish and the absence of visible feeding.

The Estaz Minnow is an abbreviated version of the Krystal Flashabugger. I "lifted" it from Lefty Kreh's *Saltwater Fly Patterns*, without giving much thought to its history. Then, after using it with success on many occasions, I learned the story behind it.

Thanks to Bill Gunn, of the Florida Council of the Federation of Fly Fishers, for setting me straight on the Estaz Minnow's interesting history. Here it is, in his words:

> It originated with a friend of mine named Ron Whiteley, when Ron and I were both members of the Thames Valley Chapter of Trout Unlimited, as well as the Connecticut–Rhode Island Saltwater Fly Fishers. Ron is an old striped bass man who was looking for a pattern that had the size, shape, and action of soft-plastic baitfish imitations like the Sluggo, which were so popular with the casting crowd during the late 1970s and 1980s. Ron Whiteley showed me and the other members of TU and the Fly Fishers what he came up with, and we used it extensively for bluefish and stripers. When I moved

to Florida in 1994, and became a member of Backcountry Fly Fishers of Brevard County, I showed it to Ron Winn.

Ron Whiteley, by the way, called his pattern the Estaz Marabou. He now lives in Rotunda West, near Boca Grande. A few years later, Norm Zeigler added plastic eyes to this pattern, which he renamed the Schminnow. By then, Ron Whiteley was already living on the West Coast and sharing his pattern with other anglers. My belief is that Zeigler became aware of it by word of mouth, and wrote a story that featured it after changing its name.

Tying the Estaz Minnow is super-simple. I start out the fly like a Flashabugger, but omit the hackle and substitute Estaz (long flash chenille) for the body. The Estaz fibers create an effect that's similar to hackle, while being much more durable. Because of the preponderance of synthetics that are used in this pattern, I use superglue instead of head cement.

I tie Estaz Minnows in chartreuse on size 2 Mustad 34007 saltwater hooks, and use them primarily as a "change-up" pattern when fishing for spawning peacocks. My favorite colors under "jungle" conditions? Purple and black, in that order, but I stick with pure black when it's snook that I'm after.

HOMER RHODE'S SHRIMP FLY, AKA SEA-DUCER

The Tamiami Trail and the creeks surrounding it figure heavily in the history of the salt marsh region—as well as southwest Florida's inshore fishing in general. Fly patterns that worked in these warrens weren't all that many, but served as bellwethers for future anglers. Today's fly fishers owe much to the tiers who helped open this region.

Sea-Ducer

- **Hook:** #2–3/0 Mustad 34007
- **Thread:** Color to match wing
- **Wing:** Saddles, at least 3 per side, tied in at the hook bend. In this version, the wing is tied "outboard" style.
- **Hackle:** Several saddles, palmered
- **Flash (optional):** Mylar

One character who helped write that history was a former game warden named Homer Rhode. He may be best known for his signature loop knot, but Rhode was also a first-rate angler and tier. Back when he ran the Miami MET, Lefty Kreh fished with Rhode on several occasions, after departing from a barge

Mike Conner's Shrimpy Sea-Ducer. Mike has fished the salt marsh since before he started writing. MIKE CONNER PHOTO

that Rhode kept parked in Chokoloskee's Barron River. How did Lefty describe these encounters? "I remember we'd go out at dusk," he told me, "and Rhode would race through those mangrove creeks and channels until we were so far gone that I started to worry. No moon to see through the branches, or markers to guide us. How he ever found his way around was uncanny."

But find it he did, and Lefty recalls one night in particular: "There was this bend where the snook were *really* popping. We caught fish after fish as soon as our flies hit the water." After catching their limit (it was four fish per angler back then), the two retraced their path and returned to the barge and breakfast—and later, a nap. Lefty recalls how the two woke up in the mid-afternoon, and how he urged Rhode, "Let's go back to that spot again." That's when Rhode—a man of few words—informed Lefty: "No way. I couldn't find it in the daylight."

Along with his uncanny ability to navigate the Ten Thousand Islands, Rhode was a shore-fishing expert, which he proved in the Tamiami Trail and other, neighboring canals. Supposedly, even before the arrival of Rocky Weinstein, Rhode was scouting the banks for snook. According to Lefty, Rhode actually discovered the relationship between snook and the squashed frogs that he found on the tarmac. Along with his other accomplishments, Rhode came up with a streamer—he called it his "shrimp fly"—that later became popular under the name Sea-Ducer. It employed a wing of flexible saddles and a hackle collar—one that was capable of pushing water, just like other successful salt marsh patterns.

I remember reading—I'm no longer sure where—about a midwestern fly fisher who tied exquisite, and effective, Sea-Ducers with thick, narrow hackles.

The Judge Allen

There's a persistent tendency among upper-class fly fishers—physicians, diplomats, military officers, etc.—to take credit for certain patterns. Names like "Colonel Bates" and "General Practitioner" are two examples—which leads to a story.

Back when my longtime pal Captain John Donnell lived in Fort Lauderdale (he owned a fly shop on trendy Las Olas Boulevard), we spent hours at the home of Jack "Bass" Allen, the archetypical Everglades fly guide. After one of our evening visits, John said to Jack: "Jack, you gave me three things!"

So, what were they?

"Small fish," said John, filled with emotion. (Jack, at the time, was planning on reprinting his business cards to include "specializing in small bass.")

John added: "The second was marabou."

The third?

"Block ice."

In the interest of further explanation: We'd sit in the shade in Jack's modest backyard, drinking Scotch on the rocks—rocks that we chiseled from a gleaming block that we kept in a cooler—until the truth was no longer in us.

So, how does this tale all come together?

Easy. Jack tied a simple but highly effective pattern from a matched pair of marabou blood plumes, a few turns of grizzly hackle, and tiny bead-chain eyes. This fly was *so* effective for so many salt- and freshwater species that John decided to name it the "Judge Allen."

An excellent choice, by anyone's standard! ■

Rabbit and marabou—the quintessence of movement! Tiny, no doubt, but even full-size gamefish can't resist it. If my memory serve me, this is the vaunted Judge Allen.

Voila! He'd hit the nail on the head. Just as I figured: The narrow profile and thick, short-barbed hackle collar achieved a result similar to a deer hair head.

Sea-Ducers can be tied in any number of color combinations. Lefty, in his *Saltwater Fly Patterns*, fully revised and augmented edition (Lyons Press, 1995), writes about tying the wing saddles "outboard" style and retrieving this fly with the slightest of movements—thereby activating all the hackle fibers.

THE BLACK MARABOU MUDDLER

One of the most effective patterns to ever grace a fly tier's vise is a Marabou Muddler tied in black, with gold accents. A descendant of Don Gapen's original Muddler Minnow, a fly designed to imitate river sculpins, the marabou version resembles a broad variety of forage, as evinced by its widespread appeal—which increases exponentially with the addition of marabou.

Black Marabou Muddler

- **Hook:** #2–8 Mustad 9671
- **Thread:** Black flat waxed nylon or Flymaster Plus
- **Body:** Gold Flashabou
- **Tail:** Fluff from the base of a red hackle quill, or a tiny tag of red wool yarn
- **Wing:** 2 black marabou "blood" plumes
- **Flash:** 2–3 strands of gold Angel Hair doubled
- **Head:** Black deer body hair

Tying Tips

Wrap the rear two-thirds of the hook shank with thread while moving from front to back. While allowing your bobbin to dangle, tear off a bunch of the fibers from the base of a red saddle hackle quill, and tie them down at the hook bend. You can even them up by tearing the tips between your thumb and fingernails.

Attach a strand of gold Flashabou over your previous wraps, making sure not to displace the hackle fibers. (Regular tinsel will also do, but it tends to tarnish and it's heavier.) Bring the tag end forward before doubling it if necessary, in order to create a uniform body, then tie it down with your thread. At this point your bobbin should be hanging at the forward extent of your thread wraps. Coat those wraps with head cement and wrap the Flashabou through it, while making sure not to leave any gaps or spaces.

When the head cement dries, apply the wing. Select two marabou "blood plumes," which are fan-shaped with extremely thin quills (I prefer black or yellow for brackish water). Grip each an inch from its tip and remove the quill (once again, with your thumb and fingernails), then moisten what's left with saliva or water. (Spit on your forearm if necessary; never put tying materials in your mouth, dyed or otherwise.) Even the tips before tying in the plumes over your previous thread wraps. I'll occasionally add a hair wing first, usually a few fibers of non-flaring deer hair. The issue here is one of proportion: With that in mind, I make all my wings one-and-a-half to two times the hook length. After adding the marabou, grab the ends of two or three strands of gold Angel Hair) before hooking the midpoint around the wing butts and tying it down while pulling the strands backward. Coat the wraps with head cement. (Note: I'll add black deer hair or squirrel tail if I'm adding an optional underwing.)

Select a patch of hollow, fine-diameter deer body hair that flares when you pull on the tying thread. Choosing the right materials is always important, and with deer hair it reaches the level of science. Snip a few hairs from the patch, and tie them down with the tips pointed backward. They should extend half the length of the body. At this point, you don't need the hair to flare, so go easy on the tension (or use hair that isn't hollow). Use your thumb and forefinger or a homemade "pusher" (a throwaway ballpoint pen with the ink supply and tip removed) to push the wraps to the rear.

Start adding hair, specifically the hollow part where it meets the skin. I add small bunches in increments and touch the wraps with head cement, and I always keep pushing them backward. After covering the shank to the hook eye, tie off the thread and cut it (I used to employ a whip-finish, but now I rely on multiple half-hitches), then remove the fly from the vise. Touch the wraps with a tiny drop of head cement, and clean out the eye with a needle.

Use your scissors to shape the head, while keeping one cardinal rule in mind: You want this fly to resemble forage that's indigenous to where you live. I keep mine streamlined, and not too bulky. When viewed from above, I want it to resemble a tadpole, not a hopper or sculpin.

This fly's goodness lies all in the action, which also relies on its ability to "bulge" or wake during retrieves. That's where the deer hair head comes in. In conjunction with the marabou, it creates the illusion of a baitfish scurrying for cover. That's the look we want here. This pattern can be tied in any color, on any size hook. Just keep it lightly dressed if you want a "waker."

I've enjoyed consistent success with both the black and yellow versions. There's one stretch of the Tamiami Trail canal where I release tarpon on a regular basis. You probably won't know it unless you fish there often, but you can find entire portions with a white sand bottom. It's possible to watch tarpon cruising these patches or, when the air is still, find them laid up directly above them. Both are great times for casting this steroidal trout fly that lands with the grace of a salt marsh mosquito.

I recall gripping a 10-pound tarpon—by its lower jaw—while removing the fly. It decided to jump, which impaled me. This is an ideal pattern for moving water—especially below spillways. While it's a good imitation of the ubiquitous black mollies that I'm constantly referring to, it's also easy to see in conflicting currents. And the bulge or wake that it leaves triggers vicious strikes from brackish or freshwater tarpon.

Poppers and Sliders

Both the noisier popping versions and their streamlined cousins work well in the tangled warrens where the Glades and inner bays of the Gulf meet. There's a world of difference between "exploding on top" and "breaking the film." Specifically, luring a fish that extra half inch through the surface is tougher than drawing it several feet off the bottom. Forget what happens when you hook a tarpon; fish, as a rule, aren't partial to air. There are times, however, when they're surface-specific and when they turn up their noses at subsurface offerings.

The slightest variation in where a fly rides may determine whether predators will attack or refuse it. Fish scan the surface during low-light conditions: at dawn or dusk, or on cloudy days. Off-color water produces a similar effect by limiting the amount of light that can penetrate. From beneath, the surface is a shimmering mirror against which surface lures show up in bold relief. Too much disturbance and the fish head for the hills (or channels); too little and they ignore whatever you're selling.

So how can you stay on track? By being conservative and moving slowly. If fish are serious about hitting on top, you'll know it. The signs include frequent concussions, from which leaping forage attempts to escape. The next is the presence of natural camouflage, be it muddy water or the previously mentioned

A foam slider resists destruction and offers ease of construction.

low light. Shallow water is another clue, since the fish don't have all that far to rise. Combine any two and you could be in business; all three and you're ready to launch. That's when snook and tarpon go on a rampage and literally tear up topwater baits.

Say you're getting frequent strikes on a subsurface pattern when concussions start erupting in the waters around you. Then, all of a sudden, the fish quit hitting. You notice that their attacks have intensified, but you'd hardly know it from the results you're getting. So, how can you turn the tide? Your luck will probably improve if you switch to a "waker," say, a Marabou Muddler or a well-greased Conehead—something that, for the most part, remains "in" the film. Then, as caution devolves into reckless abandon, what worked before is suddenly passé. That's when snook or tarpon look for something splashy: a slider or popper, usually in that order. When they completely forego their inhibitions, they'll smash a popper on every cast. However, those leg-studded monstrosities that shine in the swamps have limited value here—even to salt marsh bass. The fish seldom require more than a slider, and if they do, it's not for long.

As far as poppers, fish occasionally prefer them here in the salt marsh, when the water gets cloudy or they're feeding in run-outs. I've had marginal success with the foam-disk versions. For yeoman service, I prefer small pencil poppers made with hard-foam bodies: the ones you make from kits, like those you get from Wapsi or Bass Pro Shops. Since the hooks that are included are a bit too light, I replace them with long-shank Mustads (34011), usually in the next-larger size, after sanding the slots to accommodate the thicker shanks.

Important Salt Marsh Baits and Profiles

A tiny, well-used cichlid imitation. Juvenile oscars and Mayans are becoming a major food source. It's not uncommon for predators to feed selectively on slab-sided prey: in fresh water, on the young of both sunfish and cichlids; in the salt, on sand perch.

This 3D synthetic pattern imitates immature Mayan cichlids—common in salt marsh creeks and canals. The 3-D Minnow, a pattern used primarily in salt water, is another example of a flat, or slab-sided, fly. It's a Bob Popovics pattern that Jody Moore brought back from a New Jersey fly show. Popovics is widely regarded as one of fly-tying's all-time greatest innovators.

The ubiquitous Mayan cichlid. Snook target the small ones deep within the mangrove tangle. There's a brief period during the early spring when big snook in the salt marsh go all-out for juvenile Mayan cichlids—3- to 4-inchers—to the exclusion of just about everything else.

Baby bluegill? Sounds about right.

This tiny, accurately colored synthetic minnow apes many backwater baitfish.

The term "glass minnow" includes a mirepoix of species that inhabit both fresh and salt water. If there's a common thread (pun intended), it's that all have long, thin bodies (often wrapped with some sort of ribbing), sparsely tied wings (or no wings at all), and a wide strip of flash running down the sides just beneath where the lateral line would be located.

Mylar hollow-tube minnow. Tiny, immature gambusias, or mosquito fish, come immediately to mind.

Frogs: Unsuspecting Victims

I'm reminded of the legendary Captain Bill Curtis, and the 27-pound snook he caught on a slider while fishing the canal alongside Highway 29. Bill told me repeatedly how his old friend Rocky Weinstein (arguably the original Land Captain) would look for squashed frogs while he guided parties. Here's how Bill explained it:

Frogs, like snook, move around, and every so often they do so en masse while en route to a different marsh. While some don't make it, due to the traffic, others become fodder for snook—fish that lie in wait in the grass-lined channels. Evidence of where the frogs were crossing remained on the tarmac, which let Rocky know where snook were also waiting.

Rocky—who, according to one contemporary, couldn't read a nautical chart—drove charters around in his car (I feel a bond here), while they fished the salt marsh for tarpon and snook. At the end of the day, if he'd seen squashed frogs, he'd call Bill in Miami, who'd notify Chico Fernandez. The pair would leave Miami in Chico's Mercedes, make the 80-mile drive, and meet up with Rocky. (Lefty Kreh once told me that Homer Rhode did something similar—as far as scouting for carcasses. He *did* know both Rocky and Homer.)

The snook kept tabs on the frogs, as I mentioned, so after sunset, when the tide started falling, they'd wait in the current for more to come. By that time, Bill and Chico were already in place.

For what it's worth, I know that spot. But I've never been able to repeat the performance. I've tried plastic imitations that worked well on bass, while big snook were churning the surface, but I've never gotten so much as a sniff. The late Charley Waterman, who also knew Rocky, corroborated Bill's story. ■

Captain Bill Curtis and his 27-pounder. He caught the snook on a slider bug. PAT FORD PHOTO

I have enjoyed some spectacular fishing for both snook and tarpon with sliders—when they wouldn't hit anything else. I remember "releasing" three tarpon on a single cast—quite a feat, although strictly luck. I'd fight one to the point where I could nearly grab its lip, only to have it spit the hook. At the time, I was wading alongside a bridge.

I remember the first one letting go, and the bug falling back at my feet. Then, before I could strip out enough fly line to make a false cast, a second fish took it off the surface. I fought that one to where I thought I could beach it, before it too let go. This repeated itself a third and final time, after I'd reeled my leader into the rod guides—with a fish attached. I barely had time to take up my slack. That's three short-distance "releases" without making a backcast.

I could have probably speared one; fish were feeding that close. While gambusias and mollies ran helter-skelter, that bug was all they wanted (at one point, I actually stopped to experiment).

The one I'd hooked those back-to-back fish on was the last of my sliders. So when I finally ended up snagging it on the opposite bank, I stripped to my skivvies and swam the canal in an attempt to retrieve it. If anyone had seen me they would have called the "white jackets."

The melee lasted for nearly an hour, as the tide kept falling. I was up to my armpits in surface feeding, and willing to forego simple common sense. Since the mangrove roots were covered with hydrozoans (think baby jellyfish), my skin burned like fire as soon as I touched them.

Silent invader: A snook ghosts inland through a maze of shallow, tannin-stained water. PAT FORD PHOTO

The Suburbs

The South Florida landscape is pocked with waterways—all manner of lakes, canals, lagos, ditches, whatever the developers chose to call them—hundreds, even thousands, of acres of water, depending on who does the counting and to what end they do it. While many hold forth in ramshackle neighborhoods, their banks littered with garbage, even the worst may host vibrant populations of outstanding gamefish. Yet others that are surrounded by upscale homes and businesses also hold fish—or not.

The species you'll find in this aquatic hodgepodge vary widely and run the gamut from largemouth bass and sunshine (striper/white bass) hybrids to exotics, some unique to the area. Most of the larger lakes—and the canal systems they're part of—are accessible to anglers. This amazing fishery offers countless opportunities, with the chance to catch exotic species from faraway

Our South Florida suburbs are dotted by a seemingly endless array of lakes and waterways. The ones farthest from the Atlantic or Gulf are typically fresh or brackish. What an incredible resource! PAT FORD PHOTO

Even the tiniest, least-likely ditches often harbor hidden treasure. This is a bullseye snakehead hot spot.

Cindy Russell slugs it out with a Broward butterfly peacock. Starting in the mid-1980s, these fish fanned out through South Florida's freshwater canals.

A backyard collection of "tame" bass and bluegills. PAT FORD PHOTO

places and confront outsize fish in small, confined quarters. What more is there to ask?

The flies that produce here are, for the most part, basic patterns: streamers and poppers. That's with the exception of flies that are tied to tempt vegetarian species, several of which (the mullets) are native.

Suburban Canals

On either side of South Florida's swampy interior lies an amorphous buffer—a congested nightmare of traffic and stucco that's best known for its remorseless development. This ribbon of concrete is occasionally parted by nondescript canals—many a lot "straighter" than some politicians' agendas. As water flows toward the Atlantic or Gulf via these sea-walled conduits, it passes through a series of spillways, where it acquires a brackish and, later, a salty complexion. Here's where major changes take place in predators' diets. The spillways focus the action. This becomes more apparent after a downpour, when the gates are lifted and forage-laden water rushes downstream toward the salt.

This is where you'll start seeing larger forage: say, gizzard and threadfin shad, along with more sand perch and mullet. This, in turn, attracts much larger predators with man-size appetites. Think 30-pound snook, 100-pound tarpon, and serious jack crevalles. Gone are the days of selective feeding on tiny guppies,

Running spillways call the tune for suburban fishing. Suburban canals represent a major angling resource, especially here in southeast Florida—where some are strictly fresh, and some remain perpetually brackish.

Roan zumFelde, of Naples, Florida, is a font of knowledge on southwest Florida patterns. Here he is with his White Bait, part of his Predator series, that is tied with synthetics. ROAN ZUMFELDE PHOTO

miniature mollies, or "grass shrimp." It only makes sense that as these salty intruders work their way inland, they adjust their diets.

The transition from fresh water to salt is often gradual—and, sometimes, reversible as the tide and rainfall amounts recycle. Open spillways assure the exchange. Backyard canals may therefore simultaneously host species from both environments—say, largemouths, snook, ladyfish—à la creeks in the salt marsh.

CANALS WITH MORE THAN A HINT OF SALT

Water from the interior eventually trickles seaward. Finally, just before it reaches the Intracoastal Waterway (ICW), what's in canals is, for the most part, salty. Here forage consists primarily of mullet, small grunts, and sand perch, or—depending how close you are to an inlet—possibly shrimp, pilchards, and other "white bait." Flies that are effective here reflect the transition from brackish or fresh to salty.

I spent years fishing around bridges and in the local port facility—before 9/11 altered our nation's priorities. Most of what I did was at night, under the street-lights or the flood lamps among the ship slips. A proven technique, whenever I was able to find a shadow line, was to wait out the tarpon. Then, when the tide started falling, I'd sight-cast to fish that patrolled the line. My secret? Get your fly in front of an oncoming fish. My favorite pattern? Joe Brooks's Platinum Blonde, with the white wing and tail and a flat tinsel body.

Other fish that are prime fly-rod targets include the ubiquitous jack crevalle and that great jumper, the chiro, or ladyfish. Both respond well to saltwater poppers. In fact, just before dark, when the surface slicks over, the ladies come up to start what I call "washing." Seems that all herring-type species

Mangroves line stretches of residential waterways. They serve as shelter for many euryhaline game fish. PAT FORD PHOTO

insist on doing it—if conditions are right! During the day, the ladies go deep, but they'll break the surface and put on a show for anglers who toss them a Clouser Deep Minnow.

As far as the jacks, they're another visual target that anglers intercept when they spot a school coming their way. Jacks typically raise a ruckus when they run up and down seawalls in pursuit of forage. It's typically a fall-through-spring ritual that takes place on either tide.

Juvenile tarpon also work the seawalls, mostly on hot summer nights. While they feed on baitfish in the glow of streetlamps, they remain curiously selective in this protein-poor environment that hovers precariously between salt and fresh.

Now this you may not be aware of: When predators swim inland on the incoming tide, they typically will do so along the right bank (looking inland). They then reverse the process when the tide starts to ebb. Several respected anglers have reported this phenomenon. That being said, the patterns I fish in both extremes fit into two basic categories: those for slack water and those for moving water, regardless of salinity. For slack water I prefer patterns that feature plenty of movement: Buggers, Muddlers, fast-stripped Deceivers. My reasoning? "More bounce per ounce," where the fish have a prolonged opportunity to

Jim Grace's Snook Fly. Jim is a local legend around southwest Florida, and has contributed much to the art and science of fishing dock lights and mangroves. His ties, which are basic, produce in a variety of venues. According to Roan zumFelde, "One of our all-time greats was Captain Jim Grace's Snook Fly. You could fish it anywhere and still catch snook, redfish, and tarpon."

examine your offering. For moving water, below spillways or in culverts, the ability of a pattern to wake makes a difference. It should go without saying that Marabou Muddlers are a major go-to pattern—although when gamefish are holding deep, a weighted pattern should replace the deer hair.

The trick to fishing spillways, especially for tarpon, is to stand upstream from where you see them rolling. Then, quarter your fly down and across, and let it wake near the surface with minimal stripping. I've seen hundreds at a time rolling below spillways, but only when the current is running. That means either after a heavy downpour or in anticipation of an approaching tropical cyclone—when the authorities hope to lower the level in Lake Okeechobee.

Suburban Snook, Jacks, Seatrout, and Tarpon

A loosely defined region lies between the water management spillway that's nearest the ocean and the closest inlet. It's between these extremes, typically in

Fort Lauderdale's charter boat docks, pre-1950, on the banks of the New River. That's Captain Carl Ball's grandfather's boat, the AWOL*—a name Carl preserves in his present-day charter operation.* CAPTAIN CARL BALL PHOTO

Development crowds the banks near present-day Boca Raton inlet. Encroachment is a way of life in South Florida, but good water remains.

upscale neighborhoods, that saltwater predators ply a dizzying array of suburban canals and, of course, the Intracoastal.

Most canals of this type remain perpetually salty, except after summertime downpours that trigger spillway releases—that's when the action moves further seaward—and when, on those rare occasions, the tide keeps "falling," or pushing out inlets for more than 6 of a normal, slightly less than 12-hour cycle.

Drive through any coastal city and you smell the opulence. New Age restaurants, trendy boutiques, a surplus of golf courses—all amid an overall ambience of gentrification. The fish, in the meantime, remain blithely indifferent, as they disperse and regather in order to do their business—which consists of feeding and (in some case) spawning. Less bustle, after all, means less to disturb them.

TWO EXAMPLES: FORT LAUDERDALE AND STUART

Fort Lauderdale, Florida, is home to two "natural" rivers—short ones, albeit—that connect the Intracoastal (also once a natural waterway that separated the mainland from a long barrier island) to highlands that lie a short ways inland. In the eons that preceded recent dredge-and-fill operations, saltwater species ascended these rivers. Some still do.

Fish like snook, tarpon, and jacks still ply these waters, as well as farther downstream in the Intracoastal. The problem in fishing these waters lies more in gaining access (remember, it's someone's backyard) than in choosing patterns.

For snook: This depends on exactly where and when you find them (the rules change at night), with a major caveat: The closer the salt, the larger the pattern. Tiny Muddlers work fine just below brackish spillways, larger streamers near jetties and inlets. Mullet imitations, including saltwater poppers, also score in the larger canals. Pilchard and shrimp imitations score near docks and bridges.

For tarpon: Similar to snook, with a recommendation: Retrieve streamers and bucktails at night along shadow lines. Falling tide is usually best.

For jacks: Anything that moves—the faster the better, with size depending on what you're attempting to imitate. Saltwater poppers are also effective.

For freshwater species: Don't look for sweet-water species this close to the salt, except just below spillways. Gars are a good example.

Stuart, Florida, and its environs lie in Martin County, where the St. Lucie River meets the Intracoastal (here, it's known as the Indian River Lagoon, or IRL). Acres of grass and shell flats separate the mainland and Hutchinson Island from the sometimes-blue Atlantic.

These shallows once hosted plentiful forage—including shrimp, pilchards, and pinfish—before toxic releases from Lake Okeechobee killed off much of the grass and sent everything running. Now everyone's hoping—if we have a dry winter and the floodgates are silent—that this irreplaceable resource may, at least in part, recover.

So, say it does?

Grass flats and oyster bars provide wading opportunities in heavily populated areas "inside" both of Florida's coastal shorelines. PAT FORD PHOTO

Mike Conner's Midnight Minnow

Captain Mike Conner of Stuart is a wizard at night with fly gear. He knows the local dock and bridges like the seat of his well-used center console. I fished Stuart with Mike on a falling tide when, as they say, "it was happening"—as in 50 snook on fly in a single evening. His secret weapon? Knowing when to hit the different locations, along with his deadly invention: the Midnight Minnow. This makes Mike a tour de force in these seasoned warrens that have hosted professional fishermen for nearly a century. ■

Mike's Midnight Minnow

- **Hook:** #6 Mustad 34007
- **Thread:** Chartreuse 6/0
- **Body:** Palmered pearl Krystal Flash
- **Wing:** White SF Blend winging material
- **Head:** Hot glue or Goop adhesive
- **Eyes:** Yellow/black dome eyes

Mike Conner's Midnight Minnow wreaks havoc at night under dock lights. MIKE CONNER PHOTO

Snook: Look around bridges and docks—especially the latter, if equipped with underwater lighting. Shrimp imitations and tiny Midnight Minnows are deadly around docks; larger streamers, underneath larger bridges.

Tarpon: Either on falling tides in the deeper channels (underneath the larger bridges), or casting "bugs" (see Gartside's Gurgler) below the spillway on the North Fork of the St. Lucie River.

Jacks: Anywhere—on fast-moving poppers and streamers.

Seatrout: Once a viable fishery for wading fly fishers, who cast shrimp imitations while working the edges of grass flats. Success typically depended on water quality, which, in turn, was tied to wind direction.

Redfish: They're in here, too. Most are caught "in the blind" or occasionally while fishing dock lights. It's been my experience that the western shoreline is best.

Pompano: Occasionally sight-fished by wading anglers who cast tiny Clouser variants. Mike Conner markets flies tied specifically for pompano.

Ladyfish: Once ubiquitous, still fairly common. Sinking flies during the daytime, poppers at dusk, tiny "dock flies" at night.

Bluefish: Roving marauders that invade the shallows. Anything and everything works if they find you, or vice versa. The best indication that they've entered an area is a rash of sudden cut-offs—or reeling in fish heads.

Brooks' Blondes

When fly-fishing authority, author, and editor Joe Brooks designed these flies, he wanted a basic bucktail that was effective under nearly every condition—and that's what you're faced with throughout much of the Intracoastal. More than 70 years later, I'd say he got what he wanted. This pattern—all it consists of is a tapered bucktail wing and tail, along with a tinsel or Mylar body—is still effective wherever gamefish gather to feed on baitfish. The proportions and color can be adjusted to fit specific situations. Plus, its high-riding wing tends to dip and bob in a fast-moving current.

Brooks named his Blondes appropriately: Platinum Blonde for all-white, Honey Blonde for all-yellow, Argentine Blonde for blue over white. Why Argentine? He used this pattern on his trips to Argentina with great success for that region's outsize browns and rainbows.

This was my go-to fly when I fished the seawalls around Port Everglades (Fort Lauderdale's inlet). Whenever I'd spot a tarpon cruising my way along a shadow line, I'd try to lead him and keep my fly swimming just ahead of him in my direction. More often than not, he'd slip up behind it before twisting

Roentgen's Regret

A standard Brooks' Blonde—fresh from the vise—could hardly be perfected, or be more versatile. Yet like most young tiers, I just *had* to improve it. For once I got lucky. What I came up with was, essentially, a weighted "Blondie" that sank uniformly—instead of tipping backward or forward when descending—and worked particularly well on full-sink lines. In honor of the German physicist who made this fly possible—while laying the groundwork for modern X-ray machines—I named this pattern the Roentgen's Regret. But it's really just a Blonde bombshell! Let me start at the beginning . . .

My dentist—who has since retired—used to save me the tiny lead backings from used X-ray film. I still have a box so full that I'll never run out of them.

But more to my point: Visualize my hook in the vise, with the tail and thread wraps already in place. I use shears to trim the 1-inch lead squares into a triangle shape, and attach one corner with thread to the hook shank at the bend. I then wrap the lead forward—all the while attempting to create a tapered body—and, ultimately, secure it all in place with additional thread wraps.

Next, I take a short length of braided Mylar tubing and pull out the core. I then coat the lead underbody with an ample dollop of my thickest head cement. Afterward, I slide the Mylar tubing over the cement-soaked underbody and attach it at both ends with a few more wraps of tying thread. I then trim away any excess "snippets" before giving the Mylar a second coat of cement, and remove it from my vise and allow it to dry. Only then does it go back in my vise, where I add a tapered wing.

This pattern—which is deadly on a variety of small inshore species—performs best when fished on a full-sink line. My favorite colors are yellow and red with a gold flash over a gold braid body, and white with pearl flash over a pearlescent braid body. ■

and slurping it in. I caught (and released) literally hundreds by repeating this procedure.

But even with a premise as basic as this one, you needed a "hatch" of sorts to pull it all together—say, silvery baitfish such as pilchards passing through the light. Try casting one in the salt marsh—unless, possibly, it's a micro version—and you'll come up empty.

White Brooks' Blonde variant. Descended from an older pattern that's still effective, this version, with its faster sink rate, is especially productive.

A slightly disheveled Roentgen's Regret—my X-ray lead-wrapped version of Joe Brooks's immortal Blonde bucktail.

Basic bucktails—note this one has pearl tubing applied over the head wraps—are always in style from the sand to the suburbs—basically, wherever predators feed on baitfish.

A fly fisher cradles a butterfly peacock she caught and released in one of Fort Lauderdale's western environs.

The Exotics Invasion

By the mid-1980s, anglers started seeing and catching colorful new species in South Florida waterways. While some struck baits and lures with apparent abandon—take the oscar and Mayan cichlid—others refused to, making everyone wonder: "Exactly who *are* these fish, and where did they come from?" Or more importantly: "How will they impact South Florida's native fishery?" Both were valid questions—and both needed an immediate answer.

A group of state biologists headed by Paul Shaffland (and later Kelly Gestring) soon went to work on the problem and discovered these fish, for the most part, were cichlids—members of the family Cichlidae, a group that includes the tilapias, fish that are primarily vegetarians. No one caught the tilapias, so they continued to proliferate and, not long afterward, compete with our natives for breeding space. So, while carnivorous cichlids, like the oscar and Mayan, had a natural enemy in man, the tilapias did not. This, in turn, allowed their numbers to grow unchecked and, in so doing, threaten the local ecology.

Scene in a backyard lake in South Miami. PAT FORD PHOTO

Marty Arostegui shows off an oscar—the first exotic species to appear in South Florida waterways. MARTY AROSTEGUI PHOTO

Marty Arostegui's Midas cichlid displays unusual coloration. In their native Costa Rica, most Midas are drab, while here in South Florida, just the opposite is true. MARTY AROSTEGUI PHOTO

That's until the controlled release of a larger, piscivorous cichlid—the butterfly peacock—in 1984 put the brakes to this madness. This and subsequent stockings not only curtailed the spread of unwanted competition, but provided anglers with a rare opportunity to target an exotic South American "jungle" species right here in South Florida.

The original stockings—fingerlings that had been bred from three generations of disease-free stock—were butterfly peacocks. At least one subsequent release was of the larger speckled variety. For reasons that escape me, speckled peacocks failed to make the grade in our South Florida waterways. In fact, rumor has it that one of guide Alan Zaremba's customers caught the last two "speckleds" ever recorded—both 11-pounders—back to back on a half-day charter.

Among the other exotics that eventually showed up in South Florida waters were the Midas cichlid (in several color phases); blue, spotted, and now Mozambique tilapias; the jaguar guapote; and the *Theraps* hybrid (*Ciclas melaneura*). In general, the farther south you travel, the more species you'll encounter. But that, like most other rules here, isn't etched in stone. Take the ubiquitous grass carp, which—in the event someone has a permit to stock them—live all over the country. Lake Osborne in Palm Beach County also supports sunshine hybrids,

An angler gently lifts a grass carp. Care must be taken to avoid injuring these fish. A lip-gripping device and hand support are both essential.

while nearby Lake Ida lays claim to clown knife fish. Exotic populations act a lot like barometers: They rise and fall according to the prevailing climate.

After the freezing winter of 2010, many anglers feared that the entire exotic fishery north of the Miami-Dade/Broward County line would be a thing of the past. That, however, wasn't the case. When I visited the Non-Native Lab after that disastrous winter, Kelly Gestring, the new director, mentioned that he'd recently heard tales of knife fish "surfacing" again in Delray's Lake Ida. While the majority of exotics took a hit from the cold snap, by the time of this writing, they've all recovered.

Speaking of knife fish, that's an exotic that I've fished for on only two occasions—once in Jerry Gerardi's backyard in suburban Boynton Beach, and another time with Delray Beach guide Butch Moser. What I like most about "clowns," or "ripple fins" as they're also known—besides for their stunning appearance—is that they run just as hard in reverse as they do in forward. That's why I laughingly call them "push me–pull me's." Their jumps, by the

The carnivorous clown knife fish is an aquarium castoff that provides sport for anglers in Delray Beach's Lake Ida. According to recent reports, knife fish are spreading all the way to Miami.

Marty Arostegui hoists a bragging-size peacock. He's landed world records from canals in his South Miami neighborhood. MARTY AROSTEGUI PHOTO

way, resemble those of juvenile tarpon. Jerry now writes for the *Tallahassee Democrat*, after fleeing the South Florida rat race. At one time, his neighbor held an IGFA world record for knife fish.

Many anglers report catching these novelties on swimming lures (Ratt-L-Traps, Rapalas), but most are landed on slow-trolled, live threadfin shad—small shad at that. In fact, that's what we did it when we went with Moser. As far as the greater issue, I'm 100 percent convinced they'll hit a 3-inch bucktail or streamer. Take evidence gleaned from the time we visited Jerry Gerardi:

Pat Ford and I had a number of hookups on deep-fished streamers. The fish, which acted like the one we caught on live bait, all pulled free just before we got a good look at them—while knife fish kept rolling all around us. That's before a thunderstorm called a halt to our action.

The Vegetarian Influx

Fly tiers naturally assumed, after 500 years of spinning feathers around hook shanks, that they'd finally managed to imitate every conceivable fish food. Or so it seemed, until the arrival of plant-eating exotics, coupled with a better understanding of our own domestic vegetarians, made us rethink our game plan.

Captain Carl Ball with a grass carp. Note the gripper. CAPTAIN CARL BALL PHOTO

While purists may argue over what qualifies as fly fishing, I, and my apostate clients and colleagues, have no trouble concocting imitations of plant life.

The gamefish we're familiar with are, for the most part, carnivores—they feed on animal flesh, be it fish, crustacean, mollusk, or mammal, often while it's still alive and kicking. Vegetarians, however, present a less aggressive mindset. But judging from examples like cattle, blue whales, and elephants, a cellulose diet doesn't necessarily limit a creature's development—or cramp its style. The list of suspects includes the lumbering Amur, or Chinese, grass carp (*Ctenopharyngodon*), several varieties of tilapia (*Oreochromis* spp. and *Tilapia* spp.), and two native mullets (*Mugil*). (Important note: I include mullet in this chapter because of their vegetarian diets, but these native fish are "exotics" only in the angling sense.)

GRASS CARP

The Amur, or Chinese, grass carp was brought here from Asia. These interlopers showed up with little warning—it was as if they were conjured. I remember hearing reports of giant, carp-like fish showing up in our local waterways. Carp, I knew, were a northern species, not likely to make an appearance here, so I passed off the rumors and went on my way. At the time, I knew little about the pernicious hydrilla and the other exotic weeds that were choking our inland waters. And I knew absolutely nothing about a vegetarian fish that was supposed to control these infestations.

I'd forgotten the rumors when, on a bass-fishing trip to Palm Beach County, I spotted what looked like a mini sub. It was swimming my way down the bank. The fish was huge, and from what I could see, it vaguely resembled photographs of carp I'd seen. When I cast my popper to the oncoming fish, it reacted by bolting. However fleeting the vision, it left an impression. Then, it wasn't long afterward that I encountered something similar, but this time much closer to home. The stage was set for more comprehensive research.

My fishing for carp began with limited fanfare. I'd been casting to tarpon from a bank-side redoubt that typically yielded at least a fish or two. Then, just before noon, the breeze faltered, leaving the canal surface to shimmer like a ribbon of mercury. The tarpon, in turn, disappeared. It was just too hot and still. However, despite their disappearance, I saw swirls coming from beneath the tree limbs—100 yards down the bank. After working my way to within casting distance, I still couldn't coax a hit. Reluctantly, I sat and relaxed.

At first it was a bad move. I had to busy myself swatting fire ants, but I was about to discover what was making those swirls. I couldn't believe what I saw: There, at my feet, appeared what looked like several tarpon swimming in circles

Piling up invasive weeds on a canal bank after scouring the bottom. Local farmers feed the stuff to their livestock.

on top. By now I could taste the adrenaline. It seemed like a no-brainer until I let go with a cast. Instead of attacking my Marabou Muddler, the fish all exploded in a roiled retreat. It wouldn't have been more spectacular if I'd tossed them a hand grenade. This time, I decided to remain quietly in place. It was then that my epiphany occurred.

Berries galore! Most ficus fruit in both spring and fall. Anglers take note.

I crouched in that heat until, finally, *another swirl.* It was followed by a second. Then a third erupted and a fourth until, after a few minutes, the entire school was swirling, just like before. This time, rather than casting, I sat on my butt and watched. This would translate into years of enjoyment—although I had yet to know that.

From what I could tell, at least a dozen fish were inhaling berries that fell from a tree every time a breeze blew—which wasn't that often. Imagine an otherworldly spinner fall, but instead of trout, these fish were giants. Casting seemed futile, so I grabbed a handful of berries and threw them in the water—scaring the fish in the process. I had made it a point to see how they floated, and that night I spun deer hair until my fingers ached from pinching.

The next morning, the fish and I became better acquainted. And yes, I figured they must be grass carp. Once I learned to fish them both far and fine, I couldn't raise my rod tip without hooking another 15-pounder. By noon I was frothing.

If grass carp were Atlantic salmon, some anglers I know would mortgage their homes to spend a week in my shoes. Over a three-day period, I beached 45 of these strange-looking critters. It's no wonder my desk job suffered! Despite their lowly pedigree, grass carp are a terrific dry-fly fish. I've enjoyed consistent success with my deer hair imitations that I only recently upgraded in favor of a quick-tie molded cork version.

As a postscript, someone later told me that, around the same time, celebrated Keys guide Captain Mark Krowka was enjoying similar success with berry imitations—here in Broward County, where he lived at the time. This underscores the importance of watching both the fish and the water—whether fishing the flats or closer to home, in the suburbs—and that observant anglers end up thinking alike!

I also learned that the Florida Department of Agriculture oversees grass carp, which, technically speaking, are subaqueous cattle. They're raised for release by approved aquaculture facilities for the purpose of controlling aquatic weed infestations. I understand that a few other states have taken similar steps. It goes without saying that this widens the scope of yet another exciting fishery.

Carp-Fishing Tips

1. Most ficus trees fruit in the fall and again in the spring. However, you'll find both precocious and laggard dissenters.

2. De-barb all hooks.

3. Avoid fishing for carp when the water's extremely warm or the sun's overhead. These fish, which appear to be photophobic, are easily stressed. Recovery after releasing takes time.

Two buddies: carp in the shallows. The only carp in South Florida are grass carp, or Amur. I've heard rumors that the common variety, Cyprinus carpio, may be present west of the Aucilla River. PAT FORD PHOTO

4. Keep in mind that these fish are akin to "cattle" (they're officially under the aegis of Florida's Department of Agriculture) and that taxpayers pay for them, so handle them gently. It's illegal to possess a grass carp without a permit. They have delicate gills, so the best way to control them (while you unhook them) is by gripping the base of their tails after pinning their lower jaw with a Boga grip. Keep them cradled and in the water. Gently release them into subaqueous vegetation after pointing their noses into whatever current there is.

Carp Patterns

My initial forays into tying ficus berry patterns began with a spun hair creation that I called the Kantnerberry. Basically, it's a spun deer hair ball, trimmed flat on the bottom to insure plenty of clearance. These worked, but they were time-consuming and it also became harder for me to obtain the right colors of deer hair.

Thanks to Dr. Otto Lanz, a surgeon at Virginia Tech's School of Veterinary Medicine who will fish for practically anything (as long as it's challenging), I discovered tiny "cork" spheres, which could be coated with Avon's "Cherry Jubilee" nail polish and produce reasonable facsimiles of the actual berry. The spheres, I learned later, actually consisted of a composite of cork dust and filler—which

Pat Ross, about to release a juvenile grass carp—probably one that was recently stocked. Care must be taken to avoid injuring these fish. They play a vital role in ridding our waterways of invasive, pernicious vegetation.

the polish melted. After further research, I discovered that "real" cork balls were available online at a reasonable cost. This sped up my tying immensely.

This was the first example I'd seen of using cork balls (cork composite in the beginning) as dry flies. Dr. Lanz's discovery paved the way for a new generation

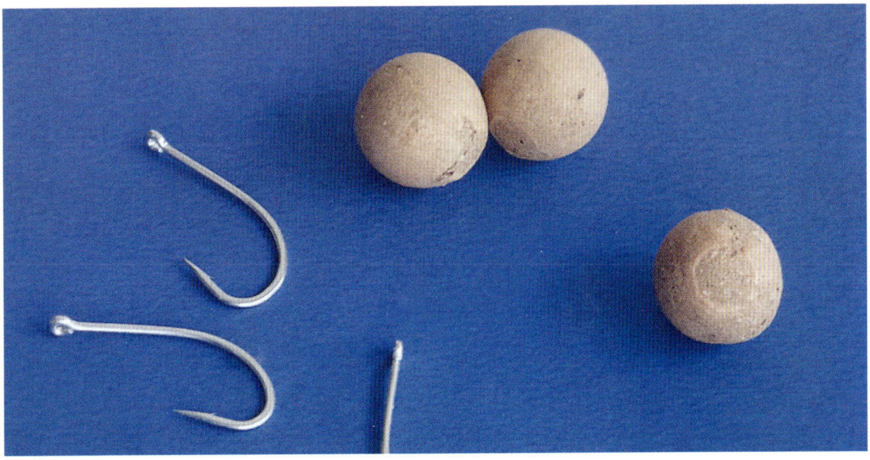

The fixin's: top-quality hooks and 10 mm cork spheres. For berry imitations, color, size, and specific gravity—how high they float—can be critical.

The author's berry trove filled with Otto's Eggs and Harlequin Duns, simply a variation of Otto's pattern with a few added splashes of yellow acrylic. Anyone who fishes the "berry hatch" knows that grass carp are finicky. Both the color and size of the berries can vary—which makes a big difference—so I started tying imitations in multiple sizes and adding a few splashes of yellow acrylic over the dried polish as a not-quite-so-ripe accent. Some days, the results can be dramatic.

Fred Ade, Grand Vizier of Griffin Road and the canals that abut it, enjoys consistent success with his version of a floating berry. It's nothing more than a Styrofoam strike indicator that he colors with a colored marking pen. This one is a proven winner against fish that are becoming more selective. It's all in how high it floats.

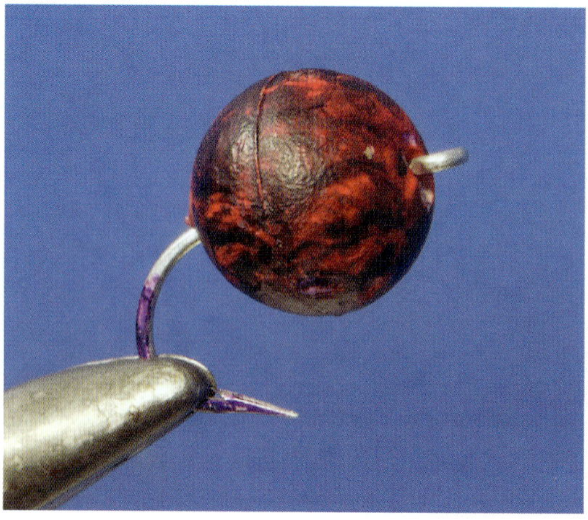

of ersatz “dry flies”—ones we now use exclusively when pursuing this species. I might add that Otto caught a fly-rod world record on one of his flies when I was the guide.

Otto’s Egg

- **Hook:** #4 Gamakatsu SC15, de-barbed
- **Body:** Cork or composite sphere, 8–10 mm diameter
- **Adhesive:** Two-part epoxy
- **Color:** One coat of Avon “Cherry Jubilee” nail polish, or a suitable substitute

Fred Ade’s Styro-Berry

- **Hook:** #2 Gamakatsu SC15
- **Body:** White Styrofoam strike indicator
- **Color:** Use a permanent marker to match the particular berries. You’ll find variations from tree to tree.

TILAPIA

The most common tilapia species—of those I’m accustomed to seeing—are the spotted, the blue, and, lately, the Mozambique. All can be found in canals

A spotted tilapia, like you find in markets. They’ll occasionally strike streamers while guarding their nests. Otherwise, feed them something reminiscent of plant life. MARTY AROSTEGUI PHOTO

Tenkara Carp

After what seems like a lifetime of writing outdoor stories and shooting photos, I have yet to sell a cover. My wife, on the other hand, takes my camera out once and—back in the "slide days"—shoots one for *Warmwater Fly Fishing*. In it, I'm bringing a carp to hand while she stands above me on a high, sloping bank. I admit that both the fishing and the posing were better then.

Here's another—this one makes me wince—although I can't stop laughing.

Several years back, the world witnessed the rebirth of an arcane technique—thanks to the Land of the Rising Sun. It's known as "tenkara," and, in the simplest of terms, it's fly fishing minus a reel. All you need is a long, limber rod (the bend absorbs the shock, thereby replacing the reel drag), a short line joined to some sort of leader—and a fly. The tenkara weighs next to nothing. With it, there's no intricate casting and no long line to manage—making it the perfect setup for kids, for female beginners who refuse to practice—or for men who, for whatever reason, don't have thumbs. Anyway, back to my story . . .

I had just recovered from "indelicate" surgery to a part of my bottom (well, near there) that had left me temporarily unable to squat with any semblance of stability. Still, I was limping around southwest Broward with my old pal Linda, who was having great fun catching and releasing bedding peacocks with a makeshift tenkara. Then we discovered a grass carp tree.

throughout South Florida. And since they're capable of tolerating a hint of salt, they're prime targets in the suburbs, or the environs of coastal cities.

If you've seen one in a market, you know how tilapia resemble a bloated sunfish—with bulging eyes. From an angler's perspective, they're a skittish adversary that seldom strikes standard baits or lures, although a few spotted tilapia figure in angler catches. While I'm not a big fan, gastronomically speaking, of this universal genus, I view these so-called panfish as worthy opponents on light tackle and tippets. But getting wild ones to bite is never a given.

A cursory examination of fresh or barely tidal canals—usually 10 or more miles from the salt—will reveal their presence. They typically hang out near breaks in the current or around sources of forage. Think the familiar ficus of grass carp fame. Also, when waterways glass over, in the early morning or just before sunset, tilapia will occasionally rise to the surface and feed on bits of floating vegetation. All nest in depressions that they scour on the bottom, with

Well, to be honest, my setup wasn't a true tenkara, but a 14-foot "bream buster" to which I'd affixed a short piece of fly line and a 20-pound tippet. Same thing, though.

Carp on a tenkara? I couldn't dismiss the vision. But on a 20-pound tippet? Remember, they're extremely wary. Could I ever get close enough to show them a berry? I was about to find out.

I inched down the bank, while gritting my teeth, and waited. And, sure enough, along came a breeze—and a berry fall. The rest is history.

I rolled out my berry, and before I could find proper footing, a huge carp grabbed it. I had just enough combined rod and fly line length to keep it from breaking me off on a straightaway run. But it, unlike its oppressor, could run down the canal sideways.

I actually managed to stop it—and turn it over a time or two—by forcing the tip way back behind me. However, now what I needed was to keep it coming—which required me regaining the bank.

But I couldn't stand up.

So I reached out to Linda, who grabbed me firmly around my middle and attempted to lift me. Meanwhile, the fish was now pulling hard in the opposite direction. The tug-o'-war lasted for three or four minutes—during which the carp used leverage to high advantage. I damn-near lost the rod once or twice (remember, I was convalescing).

Then, finally, in an act of desperation, the fish managed to pop the 20-pound tippet, causing Linda and me to fall back on our keisters. We were covered with dirt and riddled with sandspurs, yet we couldn't stop laughing. Matter of fact, I still can't! ■

those of the larger blue tilapia measuring a foot or more across. Plus, you can see the schools spook whenever they're startled.

I employ three basic strategies when targeting tilapia:

1. Chumming, either with ficus berries, small leaves, or—the perfect example of a milled vegetable product—bread or oatmeal. Then, once the fish get going, I toss them a green version of one of my mullet patterns. Spotted tilapia are extremely skittish, so make each presentation count.

2. During tilapia breeding season (late spring), I can usually induce a strike or two by jiggling a small black Woolly Bugger in front of any spotted tilapia that I see guarding their nests. After landing these fish, I'm always quick to release them as close as possible to the point where I initially hooked them. These are school fish, so why cause stress or disruption among the herd?

3. Lately, we've been catching a few Mozambique tilapia in with our grass carp, using similar methods (i.e., an artificial berry on a long, light leader).

Marty Arostegui holds up a Theraps *hybrid. What, exactly, is a* Theraps? *We're still not sure on that one.* MARTY AROSTEGUI PHOTO

A Mozambique tilapia—a fish that only recently began showing up in angler catches. They sometimes hit berry flies intended for grass carp. MARTY AROSTEGUI PHOTO

Vegetarian Piranhas: The Pacu

Of additional interest, although extremely uncommon, are occasional encounters with a fish called the pacu—essentially a vegetarian piranha. Pacus hit bread balls and berry flies, just like grass carp, and are usually found beneath ficus trees.

Once, Marty Arostegui and I were walking the banks at Hampton Pines Park in Tamarac. We'd been checking out the shoreline for snakeheads, since Marty had his eye on another world record. We'd kicked up a few grass carp that were rooting in the bottom, then all of a sudden, we saw it coming. All I could think was, *the king of the grass carp!* But as the fish drew nearer, I changed my tune. "Fifty pounds, easy," was the best I could muster, as I recognized the shape of an overstuffed permit. It looked like Igor, the pacu at the Non-Native Lab, who's been living in a tank there for 25 years.

Well, pacu it was, and a huge one. Meanwhile, I suggested to Marty that he toss it the jerk bait that he had rigged for snakeheads. Freshwater fish abide by very few guidelines; if the truth be known, most are closet omnivores. So, vegan or not, this pacu rushed over and started shaking the shad like a Jack Russell terrier. But he missed the part with the hook. Then, in a flash, he bolted, leaving behind a boil like a 300-horsepower outboard.

Typically, pacu hang out under fruiting bank-side ficus trees—à la grass carp—and grab errant berries or other vegan fare that manage to sink past their rapacious neighbors. I have heard accounts from other anglers that they will eat everything from grapes to bread balls. One thing for sure: More work needs to be done here! ■

This giant pacu lives in a friend's backyard—or should I say in the lake behind it? Pacus, for the most part, are vegetarians, although I have heard stories of ones that were caught on lures. All of these fish are aquarium castoffs. PAT FORD PHOTO

Although I've never personally done it, I hear occasional reports of fly fishers catching our ubiquitous large blue tilapia during the species' early spring breeding season by tossing tiny size 18 Pheasant Tail Nymphs into their "bomb crater" nests. I caught one once doing something similar, but on a tiny grub-tail jig. Me using a spinning lure? There, I said it—but it proves a point.

MULLET

Back in my guiding days, when I gave in to that craven lust for self-promotion, I wrote several articles about offbeat fisheries. All, I might add, generated considerable interest—sometimes more than those I wrote in support of conventional species. However contrived my efforts, my customers will all tell you that they got what they paid for—and that this was never more true than when we targeted mullet. It made for an easy day—closer to home for me. And the action spoke for itself—as in a dozen fish a day on a 4-weight fly rod, 5X tippet, and size 14 flies without renting a car at the Bozeman, Montana, airport. Do that in upstate Vermont, and they'll run you for Congress.

Dick Kirkpatrick, founding editor of National Wildlife *magazine, unhooks a small silver mullet during inclement weather. Mullet are enigmas—to be present in such numbers, yet so seldom take a hook. Well, maybe once every million casts.*

So who gives a damn about mullet? Not enough anglers, when you consider that Florida's twin *Mugil* species might well represent the greatest number of fly-catchable fish in the entire Sunshine State. Yet the indifference is understandable. Casting flies to fish that nibble at bread balls seems, well, nuts, even if these silvery rascals put up a credible fight on light gear. So what's the big drawback?

Mullet, in a word, are vegetarians. Few anglers, with the exception of subsistence cane-polers, have a clue about how to get one to hit. But that shouldn't exclude fly fishers. We already solved the grass carp riddle, which in itself

A box of tiny Antron nymphs and a popper cork round out the vegetarian species wish list.

reminds us of something: Once we start experimenting, all sorts of new species are just waiting to be caught.

Mullet aren't rocket scientists, any more than brown trout are. In fact, luring these fish is more a matter of learning where to look for them, as is discovering and imitating whatever they'll hit. Here's what makes it so tough: Since mullet are forage for larger fish, when they're in open water, they're either on the go or too nervous to feed.

Anglers who've witnessed the fall migration can testify that, while literally millions of these fish are on the move, they won't take a bait or a lure. But locate them a month or two later, when they're in a secluded canal, and the scenario changes. When they get a chance to relax, they get back to consuming—typically algae and other plant material. That's when a sleepy backwater may truly pay dividends.

Catching black or silver mullet involves finesse, since they don't just jump up and gobble your fly. Instead, they require a fair amount of coaxing, which comes in the form of chumming. "Baiting the field" with oatmeal or dry batter mix is how some folks get things started. Once mullet show up in the slick (you'll see the oatmeal flakes disappearing), ramp things up by tossing out bread crusts. That moves the action up on top.

Picture casting to schools that move furtively from bread crust to crust. That's why it's important to keep both fish and flies near the surface. Since the easiest way to accomplish this is by chumming with bread, the evolution of flies that imitate dissolving dough—and that can be suspended beneath a strike indicator—was a matter of simple deduction.

Unlike in other applications, where the indicator and fly are separated by several feet of leader, here they're closer together—sometimes within a foot or less. It follows that since the indicator floats just above the fly, the occasional fish may take a crack at it and in the process, become foul-hooked.

Of the various materials used to tie mullet patterns, white Antron (Aunt Lydia's) and polypropylene yarns are my favorites. Antron sinks slowly and has a refractive index similar to that of water: How's that for dissolving bread? Poly, on the other hand, floats—which can prove helpful late in the day.

Since the mullet fishery is defined by uncomplicated tufts of fuzz that resemble dough balls, intricate patterns with carefully constructed legs and perfect hackles aren't part of the game—but having the right-size fly is. I usually add a short tail or collar to my flies in order to enhance the illusion. Beyond that, getting a small white speck in front of hungry mullet is what matters most. Dick Kirkpatrick, an old editor friend who loved to experiment, took a fair number on Light Cahill dry flies. He'd be the first to admit that most came later in the day when floating patterns remained in the fish's feeding window longer. Nonetheless, it proves a point.

No description of fly fishing for mullet would be complete without a mention of master fly tier Frank Oblak. In my estimation, Frank, who cut his teeth in Miami-Dade and Broward Counties, was the first to tie patterns specifically intended for South Florida's vegetarian species. Thirty years ago, much of the fly fishing we do today would be considered heretical. Anyone caught with a handful of "bread" patterns might earn a trip to the loony bin. For starters, Frank carefully studied local bread-ball fishermen before fashioning patterns that looked and acted "authentic." It's from his original attempts with glitter and fuzz that I came up with the Yeastie-Beastie and her sister patterns.

Without our current knowledge, fly fishing for mullet would be next to impossible. Although anecdotal evidence suggests that a few pioneering types may have previously taken these fish on streamers, the fishery—if there ever was any such thing—died out long ago. Since no real history or fly patterns survive today, when it comes to appointing a King of the Vegetarian Fly Tiers, Frank deserves the nod.

The Yeastie-Beastie

- **Hook:** #14 Mustad 94840
- **Thread:** White 8/0
- **Tail:** Tiny length of white Antron yarn
- **Body:** White Antron, wrapped back and forth in the shape of a football and tied off behind the head after any excess fibers have been pulled back
- **Note:** A couple effective variations, the Bisquick Nymph and the MS7, are simple spinoffs of this pattern. For the Bisquick Nymph, simply pull any excess fibers downward at the "thorax" prior to tying off. For the MS7, use poly yarn instead of Antron and trim the "hackle" so that it's slightly longer.

The Carnivores

Over the past decade, we've witnessed an unequalled proliferation of exotic species—many of them carnivores—especially in the canals around South Miami. Among the new arrivals are the *Theraps* hybrid (*Ciclas melaneura*), the jaguar quapote, and the brilliantly colored Midas cichlid, a species that appears in a variety of shades. We were already familiar with the butterfly peacock, the oscar, and the beautifully barred Mayan cichlid—which is valued by some for its food value.

The carnivorous oscar was South Florida's first recorded exotic. PAT FORD PHOTO

Captain Steve Anderson, formerly of Jupiter, Florida, shows off a good-size peacock.

A jaguar quapote, a carnivorous cichlid. To me, they resemble "specks," or black crappies.

MARTY AROSTEGUI PHOTO

It all started with "Oscar" (some authorities capitalize the name), that "fern bar" favorite from the 1970s. Oscars, which eagerly suck down anything that's even remotely suspected of containing a protein molecule, started showing up in anglers' catches starting the late 1960s. Spotted tilapia and Mayan cichlids soon followed, causing even more consternation among the local bass crowd.

By the 1980s exotics were firmly entrenched. Not only did they compete with largemouths for feeding and breeding space, tilapia—since they refused to strike conventional baits or lures—essentially had no natural enemies. Hence, their unchecked numbers just kept increasing. By then, all the locals were grumbling, causing the state to seek solutions. Enter the butterfly peacock!

PEACOCKS

You may already be familiar with butterfly peacocks, a species that's erroneously referred to as "peacock bass." Actually, they're not bass at all, but cichlids, a genus with worldwide distribution. Our "butterflies"—all of which descended from three generations of disease-free stock raised in captivity from eggs donated by several South American countries—were the "magic bullet." In short, they ate juvenile oscars and tilapia, helping to restore the balance, while failing to impact our local largemouths. Paul Shaffland—who was also the first to raise a snook in captivity—and his team at Florida's Non-Native Laboratory led the charge on this project and in the process provided anglers with an exciting—if not well known in the beginning—new, nonnative fishery. That alone was unique.

From Paul's original stockings in the Biscayne Aquifer—where temperatures tend to remain stable and warmer—the peacocks spread north to Broward and, later, Palm Beach County. Some worked their way through South Florida Water Management District's (SFWMD) interconnected canal system; others were "stocked" by anglers who carried them north in live wells to their home waters. Whatever the method, the range of peacocks has expanded dramatically. Now there's talk of a population that thrives in lakes just east of Naples, on Florida's southwest coast. I've seen photos—the most dramatic? A bald eagle returning to its nest in Corkscrew Swamp with one clutched in its talons.

MIDAS CICHLIDS

The Midas cichlid, another carnivore, is arguably the most garish. Supposedly, these Central American exports are a lot less colorful in their native surroundings, but for reasons that remain unclear, those living in clear-water canals around South Miami display more lavish colors. What the Midas lacks in speed or aggression, it more than makes up for in casual indifference. Stated simply, they either will or they won't.

A Midas cichlid in full-dress array. Most exhibit drab colors early in life, then make the transition as they start gaining size. Midas are at the top of their game during spring, when they compete with peacocks for breeding space. When their "hackles are up" is the best time to pursue them.

The tiny Colorado spinner blade on the Midas-Sizer creates a commotion. The key is that it spins on the drop, which often elicits strikes from reluctant Midas cichlids.

A trick I learned while targeting Midas is what I call my "all or none rule." They either bite with conviction or totally refuse to. Picture a clear canal that was chiseled through limestone. Moving down the bank in a skiff, under the power of an electric motor, I'd see the schools laid up along the edges. They stand out like stop signs, so there's no mistaking them. But back to my premise:

I toss 'em my special pattern—I call it the Midas-Sizer—and allow it to sink. If even one individual shows the slightest interest, I begin a slow strip retrieve, interrupted with occasional pauses. Often, a school will follow and keep nipping (these fish have small mouths) until one gets hooked. If my first cast fails to evoke a reaction, it's time to move and look for new fish to target.

SNAKEHEADS

It's quite unexpected. You're stripping a bass bug for largemouths alongside a North Lauderdale strip mall, when a fish careens from the shadows and nails it, just like you'd expect a pike to devour a duckling. Unlike a pike, however, this guy turns on the boosters and bores for a pile of sunken branches—or a discarded shopping cart—that's lying there on the bottom.

Chances are he'll make it—snakeheads pack a wallop! One thing you can bet on: A spring creek this isn't!

Ever since Assistant Park Supervisor Bob Newland caught the first one ever encountered by an angler here in Broward County, Florida—remember, a similar but more injurious species, the northern snakehead, infests streams in Virginia—over a decade ago, the pundits have remained on high alert. Did

This bullseye snakehead gobbled a popper. Much has been written—some of it hype—about this dark horse gamefish. PAT FORD PHOTO

A simple deer hair and rabbit strip diver is a good choice for snakeheads. Snakeheads are also caught on sunken patterns—Mike Conner's Glades Minnow tied in all-black being a good example.

A foam diver is my favorite for targeting snakeheads. Why? Because it's virtually "bulletproof." This one withstands the snakehead's dentition and doesn't get waterlogged—two points in its favor.

the arrival of "Frankenfish"—a term coined by a Florida Atlantic University professor, since these purported "monsters" can supposedly strip a body of water of all fish life, then crawl (you read that right) on to the next one and repeat the process—signal the end of South Florida's native freshwater resources?

Not hardly.

The truth is we have a limited fishery (remember, releasing live snakeheads is forbidden by law and, in some cases, is considered a felony) that provides sport and/or food for an elite cadre of anglers. As far as crawling, snakeheads—they can survive for hours out of water—*can* use their pectoral fins for locomotion.

Most snakehead enthusiasts are addicted to hardware, but snakeheads will eagerly hit flies that fulfill certain requirements, such as swimming on or near the surface—like a frog or a baby duckling. Say you just beached a snakehead: Don't be overly anxious to put your thumb in its mouth to unhook or restrain it. The term "snakehead" has more than one meaning!

The big hurdle with snakeheads is finding one in their ever-expanding habitat that began in the C-14 system in Pompano Beach, Florida, and has since worked its way west and southward. So, how *do* you find them? First, by studying a canal map and then doing the research. They either lie on the bottom, expelling occasional bursts of air that resemble champagne bubbles, or rest in the shade while waiting for forage—which includes the young of bass and cichlids. Bass and peacocks return the favor. The second grouping is, by far, easier to target. Just

Marty Arostegui hoists a "nice" snakehead (if such a thing exists). These fish, which were once confined to a single canal system, have since moved on—causing concern among members of the scientific community and purists alike. So far, however, it seems there's been no problem. MARTY AROSTEGUI PHOTO

Marty Arostegui's frog. He likes the large surface disturbance—and so do the snakeheads.

work your way down a canal bank, while carefully working both sides and the middle. These fish are skittish, so distance is a definite advantage. Snakeheads, no matter what they're up to, prefer a fairly fast-moving fly or lure.

BARRAMUNDI

I'm sitting in a restaurant—one with a stone steer at the entrance instead of rinky-dink neon—stuffing my face with a western omelet, surrounded by wall art with titles like "Cracker Neck Tie" and featuring likenesses of men wearing cowboy hats—along with the genuine article. My companions? Try a couple of cellphone-totin' city boys—guys who'd look more at home at a Rotary meeting than bustin' cattle with the local gentry. Then there's George, my roughshod companion, who could pass as a saddlebag in a Roy Rogers rerun. These guys, Gawd bless 'em, are all my fishing pals.

We're deep in the heart of cattle country, somewhere near Keenansville, Florida, which is little more than a whistle stop on the road to bustling Holopaw. We've been rolling along Highway 441 for quite some time now, which leads me to believe that we may be near our destination. I don't dare ask for fear of exposing my "soft side" (whatever that is). Figure it's a "guy thing," but when Pat Ford's cellphone rings with a call from his law partner, we're busted. My phone is off. First, I plan on saving the battery. Plus, I welcome the chance to drink in the quiet. The vibe here is definitely different—and a lot more peaceful.

So what the hell are we doing out here in the middle of nowhere? Well, we're chasing barramundi, aka "Australian snook," and there's only one place in the state—let alone the country—where these pugnacious exotics hold forth. It's in

May all your barras be mundis . . . Marty Arostegui and I sample a bit of Oz hidden away in Central Florida. PAT FORD PHOTO

a series of ponds that lie just south of Orlando on property that's maintained by an outfit that calls itself Osceola Outback Adventures (call 407-908-3216 or visit www.osceolaoutback.com).

So, what's the big attraction? Listen up, pardner: These barras are the meanest freshwater fish this side of Australia (another major cattle producer). If you believe the rumors, they'll drag the same-size snook backward. Backward sounds good, matey. Meanwhile, who doesn't enjoy escaping to where concrete and asphalt give way to acres of green? And, of course, herds of cattle—and hard-fighting gamefish.

We finish breakfast and leave. And not long afterward, we see a sign on the right that reads "Hennecy Lane" and turn off the highway. The first thing I notice is Byron Hennecy's vehicle, which begs the question: What must he think of four dudes rollin' up his gravel driveway in a Cadillac Escalade, all of us wearin' moisture-management shirts that are festooned with the trappings of some goofy contest? Not to mention that we're packin' more fly-fishing gear than a Jackson Hole fly shop.

So here comes Hennecy, toolin' up in a camouflaged golf cart. In addition to a cooler filled with drinking water, the cart sports several rod holders, a

Byron Hennecy, with Marty Arostegui, shows off a fat barramundi. PAT FORD PHOTO

Kimberly Hennecy samples this year's crop. It's a new beginning for her and her husband.

BYRON HENNECY PHOTO

varmint rifle, and a shotgun. Each rod holder carries a spinning or casting rod rigged with a lead-head/grub combo. As far as bait-casting tackle? Today we're "Brothers of the Angle."

After a brief introduction, Hennecy, who guided Marty on a previous outing, indoctrinates us in the fine art of mundi fishing, which consists of casting a lure into the tailrace behind one of several paddles—they aerate his ponds, while creating a current—and retrieving. Once George hooks up, Hennecy figures it's safe to escort Pat and Marty to the opposite bank, where either the fishing or the light—or both—is better. That suits them thar rubes immensely.

The action for all of us shifts into overdrive.

At one point, I stop casting and watch Hennecy work a topwater plug. The mundis approve, so I rig a saltwater popper on an 8-weight outfit spooled with a floating fly line and start flailing away. The fish are on it as soon as it hits the water, but only if I cast it the requisite 70 or 80 feet into fast water and strip it just right. I miss several fish in quick succession, and end up scorching my fingers. Eventually, however, one stays hooked. I wrestle it to the bank, where I easily remove the barbless hook and release it unharmed.

It finally hits me: Whoever clued me in to this spot really nailed it. They *do* look and fight like snook on steroids. The action continues for several hours, forcing me to race back and forth between Pat, several cameras, and my fly rod. Work goes into any photographic project, but we're having fun doing it.

As far as the future, the mundis are grandfathered. Someone stocked fry in several ponds on the family plot and the rest, so to speak, is history. From a sport-fishing standpoint, the effect was dramatic, and while preservationists turn a jaundiced eye toward the introduction of *any* exotic, a more pragmatic approach might be to ask, "What took you so long?"

My friends, I suspect, are among the latter.

Actually, the barramundi situation is a lot like what we face in South Florida with our butterfly peacocks: Both species exist at the behest of environmental factors (in the case of barramundi, they can't reproduce without brackish water, and the spread of both is severely limited by temperature). That notwithstanding, exotics provide "filler" in ecosystems that have either "gone south" due to pollution or development, or are artificial to begin with.

Limited spread? As a case in point, the back-to-back freezing winters of 2010 and 2011 wiped out Byron's entire operation. But as of the fall of 2017, he's back in action.

So how do I feel about fish farms in general? That depends on many factors, but if you haven't noticed, half the fish we buy these days in the market is

Bob Clouser's Deep Minnow

This familiar pattern, first tied by Bob Clouser of Middletown, Pennsylvania, is recognized universally as *the* go-to pattern whenever fish run deep. The original recipe combined a bucktail wing and tail with a thread-wrapped body and a set of dumbbell eyes—and little else. The Deep Minnow has prevailed against practically every imaginable species—which is quite an endorsement. But it must have drawbacks, right? That depends on who you talk to.

I don't see adding a wee bit of weight as creating a jig—like the term "jig" denotes evil. We do, after all, use sinking fly lines. Meanwhile, what the weighted eyes do nicely is allow anglers to "nod" the Clouser—like certain baitfish do while nibbling at the bottom.

Standard Clouser Deep Minnow. This pattern has caught nearly every imaginable species. It's the all-time favorite among anglers pursuing peacocks—although, personally, I'm a Woolly Bugger fan.

referred to as "farm-raised." That includes barramundi, and this is a fish farm. Get the connection?

Rather than pontificate, I'd prefer to loosen my tie and laugh at four city slickers who just enjoyed a day of fabulous fishing—on the banks of a Central Florida cow pond.

In conclusion, I compare Hennecy's operation to a well-run dude ranch, where enthusiasts of all skill levels can enjoy a day outdoors while catching and releasing a formidable gamefish—with the odds in their favor. Although the chance

Some purists view it differently: Take how Jack Allen was working the banks of Florida's St. Johns River, when he found himself surrounded by what he later referred to as "serious shad fishermen." American shad hold deep in the current—hence the need for weight. Jack surmised correctly that this was a fly club outing.

Jack was casting an 1/80-ounce jig head, to which he'd added a wisp of marabou, all on fly gear—and, apparently, was doing quite well with it. Soon he was approached by another angler—apparently the organizer of the event—who asked to examine Jack's "lure."

"You know that's not *really* fly fishing," remarked the worthy.

That's when Jack took a look at his accuser's "fly," tied with its hefty dumbbell eyes.

"Not really fly fishing? What do you call this 1/32-ounce dumbbell you have lashed to *your* lure?" Jack chided, adding, "Meanwhile, my little jig head weighs less than half that." Needless to say, Jack's rejoinder was summarily dismissed as the ravings of a heretic. Rather than argue, Jack simply ambled off down the bank a bit, where he continued catching shad on his bastardized jig fly.

Another widespread application of this popular pattern here in South Florida is for butterfly peacocks. Anglers not only toss Clousers to bedding peacocks, but to their schooling cousins that are patrolling shorelines or hanging out around breaks in moving current. For peacocks, chartreuse remains the favored color (Lefty Kreh once advised me to combine "green" and "yellow" chartreuse for maximum impact).

Something I found helpful—especially when guiding anglers who lacked experience when it came to fishing high banks—was to tie up a few Clousers on Owner Mutu light offset circle hooks. If a peacock so much as touched their fly—and they couldn't tighten in time—the Mutu would catch in the corner of the fish's jaw. Then, when they finally "got tight" to the peacock, the added tension would complete the transaction. Another fringe benefit? Fish hooked on circle hooks are normally easier to release than those caught on regular J-hooks. ■

of failure may seem limited, you'll need at least some skills to be successful—enough, in fact, to make it interesting.

That's where Byron Hennecy excels. I'd recommend him and his operation to anyone with an interest in sport and relaxation. If there's a moral, it's in knowing that in the final analysis, "all's fish that comes to the net." By the time a few hours had passed, all four of us were soaked with sweat and our forearms were pumped, and not from answering cellphones.

Hennecy, who also fishes the St. Johns River for bass—and offers bow-fishing trips from his airboat—is "pumped" about his new crop of barras. In an age when Nature no longer seems capable of supporting either food or gamefish, they (and he) may well represent the wave of the future.

"Anything a snook will hit," said proprietor Byron Hennecy of Osceola Outdoor Adventures, when asked about flies for barramundi. He suggests Clousers and Deceivers, as well as basic bucktails and streamers.

Colorful Clouser. Suggested patterns for barramundi include Clousers and Deceivers in white or yellow and, as I discovered, standard-size saltwater poppers. Barras, we learned, prefer bright colors.

The Beaches

There's nothing quite like it—scanning clear water for cruising gamefish, while bathed in sunblock and breathing in salt air and the scent of seaweed. And once you get that hookup, there's no denying that "one from the sand is worth 10 from the boat." Choose any beach and you're sure to find it: that narrow ribbon of surf between the high- and low-water marks. It's in this abbreviated expanse of shallow water—in some ways, much like a shell bank or mudflat—that predators cruise in search of forage.

Picture a typical scenario: It's just past noon and the tide is rising, while you slog your way toward a copse of palm trees. The harbinger of a nasty downpour is filtering the sunlight and stifling the breeze, leaving you all alone with good visibility. You've been scanning the water close to shore, and so far, nothing. Then you spot them.

Frightened mullet signal the presence of predators. These fish make an annual fall migration along East Coast beaches—and to a lesser extent, south in the Gulf. PAT FORD PHOTO

There, headed in your direction, swims a squadron of snook—maybe 20 individuals. You quickly strip out fly line—I prefer an intermediate or slow sink weight-forward taper—into your stripping basket, after which you make a hurried backcast. Your fly lands just ahead of and slightly beyond the lead fish, so you make the correction. For the briefest of instants, you lose sight of both your fly and the fish. Then, everything comes back into focus, as two fish break from the school and lunge at your lure.

With a flash and a swirl, one's off and running. After a spirited romp that takes you into the backing, you gain control and ultimately beach him. A nice 8-pounder, bright as a just-minted dime. You unhook and carefully release him. (Note: Snook this size are inevitably males; those 12 pounds and over are typically females.)

Miles of fishable water extend along even the most populated stretches of the Florida peninsula. Some beaches, no doubt, offer better fishing than others. Still, although largely ignored until recently, any that are even remotely accessible offer savvy fly fishers solitude, as well as assorted quarries.

The key to success in the surf? First, know what you're planning to target, and match the forage they're most likely to prey on. Also, learn all you can about the effect of the tides. The surf is capricious and subject to both local and offshore

The author scans the shallows in search of a snook—on which to put his Deceiver to use.

PAT FORD PHOTO

A storm moves offshore over Hutchinson Island. See the birds and bait in the foreground? Looks like something's about to happen. PAT FORD PHOTO

weather disturbances, so keep an eye on the forecast. Also worth noting is that fish feed closer to shore at sunrise and sunset, and during the last three hours of incoming tide and the first two of outgoing.

Surf fishing, no matter how or where you pursue it, is largely seasonal, with "run fish" like bluefish, Spanish mackerel, and pompano arriving in the fall, in the company of assorted migrating baitfish and less popular predators—small jacks, blue runners, and ladyfish included—and at the top of the food chain, sharks and huge tarpon. Then, in summer, snook and an assortment of smaller predators arrive. All will take flies under ideal conditions.

The surf—or in this context, beaches in general—fit into two major categories. In the Northern Hemisphere, those located on the western periphery of large bodies of water—say, the Atlantic Ocean—experience more wind and wave action than their eastern counterparts. Take the surf at Hobe Sound or Palm Beach, compared to Sanibel or Captiva Island, or how about Florida Bay? The former are known as "high energy" shorelines, with their windswept beaches, a persistent chop, and, possibly, the threat of ground swells. It's wave action, along with wind and current, that orchestrates shoreline fishing. The same holds true in the Gulf, where the more tranquil scenario sets a different pace. Wind and waves typically work in conjunction to push volumes of water along both coastlines in what hydrologists refer to as the "longshore current."

Fish—at least, migratory species—move with the current, while periodically slowing down to feed both with it and into it. Along Florida's Gold and Treasure Coasts—thanks to the proximity of the Gulf Stream and prevailing southeasterly winds—the current flows north. Occasionally, however, it can turn around when the breeze shifts into the north. A typical nor'easter—in fact, any north wind—can transform the surf from a millpond to a maelstrom in a matter of hours.

When cold fronts pass during winter, ground swells form in the Gulf Stream, before crashing ashore on unprotected beaches—that means anywhere north of Hillsboro Inlet (Pompano Beach). It's the accompanying surge that brings the fish sometimes quickly and in incredible numbers. Just the opposite happens in spring; however, without all the drama. Rising temperatures act as a trigger, but inshore waters may take weeks to recover from winter ground swells. Then, once the prevailing breeze settles into the east, migratory species begin their retreat to wherever they'll spend the summer. It's their subsequent replacement by snook, big jacks, and returning tarpon, along with huge schools of baitfish, that signals the return of summertime fishing. It's a sequence that historically defines the nearshore realm: an area referred to as the "littoral zone." Here, along with the sand and the seaweed, you'll find fishing piers, inlets—and the jetties that frame them.

Surf fishing with fly gear—if you wish to be successful—requires specialized equipment, starting with a suitable stripping basket. You'll also need a chest, back, or waist pack to transport your flies, tools, and leader material—and lest I forget, plenty of drinking water. Special thick-soled beach shoes are another good bet, with all the trash that washes ashore these days. And don't forget that hat, a long-sleeved T-shirt, and plenty of sunblock.

When you end up miles from where you started, it's just you and the seagulls. Of course, if you want fish for the cooler, don't forget to bring one. (I drag a specialized surf cart equipped with giant Wheeleez soft rubber tires.)

The Bait

Identifying the forage, and tying effective imitations, opens new vistas for beach-going fly fishers. This isn't graduate ichthyology—far from it—just a natural extension of walk-in fishing. What it is, rather, is learning to identify sizes and shapes of a few basic baitfish—and possibly, a crustacean or two. You too can do this by simply (1) watching the sand where you're walking, as well as the water; (2) checking the high-water mark for any undevoured baitfish that may have washed or been driven ashore as the result of predator activity; or (3) seeing what captured fish cough up.

"Matching the hatch," as they say, also applies to baitfish.

This specialized Clouser is designed for targeting Spanish mackerel—which frequently show up in the surf. MIKE CONNER PHOTO

Let's start with baitfish. Something worth considering is that fish have preferences as far as what they're eating, based in part on the prey's ease of capture. The Spanish mackerel, for example, is a "slasher"—he wants something thin and round that he can slice and easily swallow, like a bay anchovy or "glass minnow." I like anchovies in my Caesar salad; it just wouldn't be the same

A wool-head streamer is just the ticket whenever mullet run the surf. Once again, it's all about "pushing water."

without them. I wonder if the macks feel the same about 'chovies as I do. Kinda makes you wonder.

Meanwhile, a snook or tarpon—who gulps instead of chews his dinner—is more inclined to inhale a hearty herring or pilchard, or, if one crosses his path, a fat, juicy "sand shiner." When it comes to baitfish, soft is invariably a sales point.

There's a third option and it comes in the form of a fat-headed mullet: something most tiers imitate with wool-head patterns. Wool heads can be highly effective, especially when mullet are "running"—as they do in the fall. If wool heads have a drawback, it's that they quickly absorb water, making them heavy and unwieldy to cast.

Your options? Either long and slender, slightly more slab-sided, or capable of popping or pushing water (remember the salt marsh). While tiers continue to turn out "miracle patterns," a selection of basics, as well as different styles of tying, is usually sufficient to cover the bases. My quick picks are:

1. Surf Deceiver, in various degrees of sparseness
2. Surf Clouser, a beefed up version of the Clouser Minnow in various weights and wing colors
3. Winn's Thread Herring, both versions
4. An effective glass minnow imitation
5. A few full-size saltwater poppers
6. Several large wool-head streamers, for when the mullet are running
7. A small crustacean imitation for pompano, whiting, or croakers when they're foraging in the curl for mole crabs. Roan zumFelde of Naples carries a

The Appel Super Flea is both effective and an innovative example of imitation. The name suggests a mole crab, or sand flea. "I named it for my late uncle," says its creator, Roan zumFelde. "He was one of the first to use fake fingernails to tie with. His nickname was Bobby Apple."

fly with a shell back that he saves for this and similar occasions. "It's the Appel Super Flea," Roan, who got the idea of tying flies from artificial nail extensions from his uncle, Bob Appel, tells me. "We use it on the beach, as well as in the backcountry, but [in a neutral coloration] it's better on the beach." It's a great sand flea or small crab imitation that works on reds, snook, seatrout, and pompano. He's even used it to catch bonefish in the Bahamas.

LEFTY KREH'S DECEIVER

In its various incarnations, Lefty Kreh's signature pattern has caught practically every species that swims in both fresh and salt water. By matching materials according to the shape and color of the local forage, tiers employ Lefty's basic template to imitate a wide range of prey. The Deceiver's appeal lies in its teardrop-like shape—bulky in front, with long, flexible wings—that's a match for most baitfish.

Lefty's Deceiver

- **Hook:** #2 Mustad 34007
- **Thread:** White 3/0 Monocord
- **Wings:** 4 to 8 saddles tied as a tail
- **Flash:** A few strands of pearl Krystal Flash
- **Collar:** White bucktail—more on the top and bottom, less on the sides

- **Cheeks (optional):** Pair of mallard flank feathers
- **Note:** This is another pattern that I'll sometimes tie slightly back from the hook eye—thereby giving myself more metal to grab for leverage. That's helpful when I'm unhooking a snook. The Mustad 34007 is my all-around go-to saltwater hook; a size 2 does a good job of imitating the small pilchards that frequent the surf. I occasionally add a pair of mallard flank feathers—one per side—that I'll coat with head cement (or Hard As Nails). Then, after the cement dries, I'll dab on a pair of acrylic two-color eyes before coating each cheek with clear acrylic lacquer.

Anglers all have their favorite Deceiver recipes. Mine's a size 2 all-white version rimmed by a pair of inboard grizzly saddles. Once a snook sees it, I get few refusals. Deceivers are good imitations of any number of baitfish. I believe that the stripes on the outer hackles create the illusion of scales on a fleeing pilchard.

This Deceiver variant was tied to resemble a cigar minnow.

Lefty's idea was simple: Create a baitfish imitation with just enough wiggle that's easy to cast and has plenty of bulk when seen from the side. That's what he did when he paired saddle hackle wings—usually tied "inboard"—with a thick bucktail collar. Lefty's Deceiver, as with other universal ties, represents as much a style of tying as a single pattern.

The Deceiver has proven extremely effective for snook on the beach. When I tie it to match the ubiquitous pilchards, thread herrings, and other so-called white bait that invades the surf during summer, it's one of my favorites, if not my number one choice. I tie it in all-white, with a single grizzly saddle in each wing half. And I paint eyes on this one.

RON WINN'S THREAD HERRING

Titusville, Florida, CPA Ron Winn ties a series of accurate and functional baitfish imitations that he fishes in the surf, the Indian River Lagoon (IRL), and the nearby St. Johns River (for the latter he ties, in his words, "a decent shiner imitation"). One pattern that I've used to advantage is what I've begun calling "Winn's Thread Herring." He ties two similar versions: one on a standard hook, the other on an inverted Kahle hook. Ron relies exclusively on synthetics when tying these patterns, which puts the onus on anglers to impart the action.

Ron likes to fish streamers deeper than other anglers but he's not into snags or using a weed guard, so he picked up the idea of using Eagle Claw Kahle hooks from watching bait fishermen fish the surf for pompano. He likes the Kahle design for several reasons. It allows him to fish around rocks in the surf, docks in the IRL, and mangroves and deadfalls without going fishless.

Ron Winn's J-hook version of his Thread Herring. Note the wing's nearly perfect taper.

Winn's Thread Herring—inverted version. This one, according to its designer, is the more weedless version.

Bend-back hooks were long considered the appropriate solution but, as Ron told me, "Traditional bend-backs frequently don't ride right, or if they're tied on long-shank hooks, they won't hold fish once you hook them—if you ever do." As far as hooks, he prefers offset models, which he straightens after first examining them and deciding where, exactly, the offset is centered. He also recommends using straight-shank models, "on which you can bend a ¼-inch platform to tie on."

Winn's Thread Herring

- **Hook:** 1/0 Gamakatsu 514
- **Thread:** .006-inch-diameter mono
- **Wing:** Crinkly synthetic, such as Ultra Hair, stacked dark over light
- **Flash:** Krystal Flash
- **Eyes:** Decal
- **Coating:** Epoxy or acrylic
- **Note:** According to Ron, "I very rarely trim the materials once I attach them. By doing some tapering in my hands, I find that the fly looks and performs better."

SURF GLASS MINNOWS

Anchovy? Silverside? How 'bout just plain ol' "rain bait"? Nowadays, the term "glass minnow" is applied so indiscriminately to so many thin, transparent baitfish that their proper identities have been blurred in the process. Here in South

Florida, surf anglers are generally referring to the bay anchovy—which appears in huge schools along beaches during the last days of summer.

Larry's Surefire Snook Fly

- **Hook:** #2 Owner 5114—101 Mutu offset circle
- **Thread:** Flymaster Plus, color to match the wing
- **Wing:** Stacked synthetic, green over white
- **Head:** Coat with 5-minute epoxy

Saltwater predators, typically, are opportunistic—until they become glutted on any slow-moving forage that can't escape their onslaughts. Take the windrows of glass minnows that become trapped in the surf by Spanish mackerel, tarpon, snook, or, occasionally, false albacore—what we here in Florida erroneously call "bonito." That's when having the "right" imitation makes all the difference. A long, skinny streamer or bucktail, tied with a broad strip of flash that extends down both sides to just short of the tip of the tail, is usually sufficient. There *are* times, however, that surfeited feeders look for exact imitations.

Selective surf fish? An indelible reminder of this frustrating phenomenon—it lasted several weeks—took place several years back on the beaches of Hutchinson Island. Every morning, just after daybreak, schools of false albacore would leave their homes on the reef in order to invade the shallows—and feed on tiny

Larry Dringus's modified glass minnow with the offset circle hook. Larry ties this pattern on Mutu light offset circle hooks, which he claims gives him a better hookup ratio and fewer cut-offs. "The hook always ends up in the jaw hinge," he says. "That lets me use lighter tippets—and get more hits in the process." PAT FORD PHOTO

A selection of Surf Candies. This pattern is the brainchild of Bob Popovics. During the tying process, Popovics layers several shades of Ultra Hair (a crinkly nylon fiber), along with strands of Krystal Flash, and then coats the bodies with epoxy. PAT FORD PHOTO

A perfectly tied Surf Candy—Jersey tier Bob Popovics's creation. Surf Candies can be tied to resemble practically any species of baitfish, but they provide an extremely accurate profile of a "skinny Minnie" with near-total indestructibility.

Larry Dringus booms one out in the Broward surf, while prospecting for snook. I've known Larry for years, during which time he's caught more snook from the surf than any local I know of—at least, on flies. PAT FORD PHOTO

baitfish. During the peak of the action, which occurred just after 7 a.m., they became so glutted that they'd refuse all our offerings. How many fish came within casting range? I watched a tiny wave break and recede alongside me, leaving three behind flopping. They literally swam up to our rod tips, so I knew they saw our offerings—yet nothing!

To solve the problem, at least partially, we'd find out ahead of time, from the previous day's reports, where the bait schools were holding. Then, we'd arrive before sunrise and take up positions. At the first hint of daylight, we'd see ballyhoo and flying fish on a mad dash for the shoreline. That's when we'd take aim on the albies—by casting beyond the tightly packed glass minnows.

BOB POPOVICS'S 3D MINNOW

At one time, I tied this pattern specifically for false albacore, king mackerel, and various reef species, as well as true deepwater pelagics such as mahi-mahi. Since then, it has proven equally effective wherever gamefish target fat, slab-sided forage, in salt or fresh water.

Local tier Jody Moore first saw this fly tied by Bob Popovics at a fly-fishing show and immediately saw its potential for South Florida fisheries. "I was impressed by Bob's ability to shape a fly so that it looks like a fat, slab-sided baitfish such as a pilchard, a pinfish, a sand perch, or, in fresh water, a Mayan cichlid," Moore says. He had frequently expressed frustration with natural materials—feathers and bucktail in particular—that "might look good in the vise, but in the water, collapse into something that doesn't match what I'm trying to imitate."

3-D Recipe

- **Hook:** 1/0 Mustad 34007
- **Thread:** White Danville's flat waxed nylon
- **Tail:** Ultra Hair, color to match that of the baitfish
- **Wings:** Ultra Hair (four or five successive applications of dark over clear)
- **Flash:** Pearl Krystal Flash
- **Head:** Epoxied
- **Eyes (optional):** Painted or decal

Another advantage to this stand-up pattern is the tier's option to add color with Sharpie markers, or create bands, stripes, gills, dots, and shadings that match that of a particular forage. Plus, the 3D Minnow won't absorb water. Then there's the durability factor, which—when tied with Ultra Hair—is high in the stratosphere.

Natural or synthetic? The 3-D baitfish clone offers the best of both worlds—and, like its namesake, can be shaped to "match the hatch."

Saltwater Poppers

Popper fishing can be extremely exciting in the salt, whether casting to a school of ladyfish rolling in the surface at dusk or blasting blues in the surf. My most outlandish application of an oversize popper from land? How about when I'd cast to giant jack crevalles off the seawall in West Palm Beach? I still had a few double-hooked billfish flies that I'd tied back in the 1990s—in hopes that I'd get a chance to use them. No dice.

But what I *did* uncover was an offbeat fishery where, for maybe an hour after daybreak, these bruisers would run the seawall in search of monster red-roe mullet. They were looking for 3-pound forage, and that's all they wanted. No 3/0 Gallasch poppers or Bob's Bangers. But what did trip their trigger was a 14-inch billfish streamer stuffed head-first into a whittled foam chunk.

The hits were, shall I say, explosive? And the sight of several 30-pounders in hot pursuit was the stuff of legends. Then the city came along and shored up the seawall with limestone boulders. Now the mullet had a place to hide—and the jacks got their walking papers. It was great while it lasted, and it would have never started

Tricked by a popper, when the school quit eating streamers. How big is this jack? No tellin'—I promptly released it. I can't forget that time when Andy Mill and I, based on a tip, were able to run down a school of monsters just off Hobe Sound Beach. Several we boated—we ended up using poppers—weighed in excess of 35 pounds. All were a workout on fly gear!

without those giant streamers that morphed into poppers—with the help of a few do-it-yourself popper heads.

While most saltwater species respond best to a size 3/0 or larger popper, there are exceptions. One is when you're chumming for Spanish mackerel with dead glass minnows (remember, macks *do* enter bays and inlets, where shore-based anglers *could* theoretically chum them—say, from docks or catwalks) and the schools eventually turn dour. Under those conditions, a well-placed pencil popper that's allowed to lie perfectly still on the surface will bring them a-runnin'. Move your bug for an instant and they'll totally ignore it. Leave it rest, however, and they charge up and blast it. It's like popping for bluegills on steroids. ■

Poppers can be fashioned from any number of buoyant materials—including Styrofoam, balsa, and my old favorite, cork. However, whenever the forage I'm attempting to imitate reaches 5 or 6 inches, I go with balsa.

A large foam slider offers another big-fish option. The use of soft foam adds to this pattern's resilience.

According to Moore, "The skill comes with the trimming, while the fun and creative parts lie in the final touches that you make with the Sharpie. You can also use epoxy to create larger heads or secure decal eyes, making this fly even more indestructible."

Land Sharks

It's as regular as clockwork: The local media reports sharks in the surf—huge schools of 'em, in fact—and footage shot from drones and choppers makes it all the way to national outlets. All these cold-blooded killers where tourists are swimming? Surely we're doomed!

This annual ritual takes place primarily off Palm Beach and Martin Counties, where the peak season runs from February through April. That's when several species of selachian tough guys—primarily blacktips and "spinner" sharks—swarm the surf for the purpose of spawning. But that's not all they do here. In a word, they attack all types of forage—specifically, schooling species like bluefish and pompano—but once the sharks' "blood is up," they don't make distinctions. The sharks swim close enough to the beach on a regular basis to be a target for anglers armed with the right fly gear.

Fly-caught shark on a beach. Surf fishing for sharks with flies is becoming increasingly popular for anglers desiring a workout.

PAT FORD PHOTO

Make no mistake, shark attacks, including those blamed on spinners, are far from unheard of. Lifeguards post warnings and, if needed, clear the surf when they sense danger from sharks or other "hazardous sea life" (for example, Portuguese man-of-wars). Moral of story? Enjoy your fishing—but don't be a hero.

Renowned fly fisher Andy Mill and I pursued sharks from skiffs on numerous occasions—as has Captain Scott Hamilton (of Jupiter), who helped develop this fishery—just yards from

One-trick pony? This huge, high-capacity fly outfit is rigged with a large orange shark fly. Why orange? To imitate a chunk of bloody jack or bonito? I used to think so—but now I wonder. As a rule, sharks prefer brighter colors—if the lure's near enough to the surface for the color to show through. (Certain wavelengths of light penetrate deeper than others.)

PAT FORD PHOTO

the surf. Famed photographer Pat Ford also gets in on the action—both here and in the Florida Keys. Pat holds, or at one time held, a tippet record for a tiger shark—another matter entirely. Both he and Mill are also accomplished tiers, and the tricks they've mastered are in many ways similar.

What we've all learned from our efforts is that spinners, especially, behave more like mainstream gamefish and less like the bottom-hugging, demersal scavengers that the general public thinks of when the word "shark" is mentioned. Instead, spinners are dervishes! Their reel-scorching runs and aerial antics set them worlds apart from other 6-foot fly-rod targets—even the vaunted "silver king" and its beak-wielding cousins. Plus, there's the added challenge of preventing cut-offs that result from all the constant writhing and chafing that takes place on those jumps. So, carry plenty of flies! Spinners hit them with gusto—especially the orange ones, as well as poppers—if they're in the mood, and if the angler knows how to work his or her lure accordingly.

In the boat, we tweak the shark's mood by chumming, and only cast to fish that show signs of aggression. It works like a charm! But since this book is about fishing from shore—or while wading, which for sharks is highly inadvisable—you need something to put the odds in your favor. How about the Law of Large Numbers?

I've witnessed many a day when school after school of spinners ran the surf in succession, all in pursuit of forage. I was casting plugs at the time and on several occasions the sharks cleaned out my tackle box. So, what about the chances of hooking one on a fly? I'd say "no problem," but since I'd leave my fly gear at home back then (the sharks' appearance was unexpected), I'm unable to prove it. My final thoughts on the matter? Since I've beefed up my resolve—along with my knowledge of the tides and weather conditions that are most conducive—and upgraded my equipment (super-big fly reel, better stripping basket), landing a shark from the sand seems not only doable, but well worth trying. However, there will be drawbacks.

On the beach, for example, you don't have that "home-field advantage" that a boat offers. Take chumming, for example. Toss out a carcass and it's swept away by the waves and current before you can make a backcast. Still, you have cards in your favor. Say, if a shark swims within casting distance, you know it's there for a reason: feeding.

Your target may have chased a bluefish or mullet—you name it—into the shallows, nearly up on the sand on occasion. But more often than not, its quarry escapes it. So you now have a *qualified* prospect. The next part is easy: getting your fly in front of an *oncoming* target—the perfect presentation!

As far as getting hookups? A shark's eyes sit far enough back on its head to prevent it from seeing what's directly in front of it. So, when a shark rushes its quarry, it rolls back its eyes and inhales (or chomps) what, a millisecond earlier,

Lump in your throat? A lemon shark tracks a fly. PAT FORD PHOTO

Rage incarnate! This shark reacts to a fly he chomped on. PAT FORD PHOTO

An assortment of shark flies. Notice they're all the same color and variations of the same basic theme? I'm not sure of its official moniker, but everyone calls it the Keys Shark Fly. Essentially, it's an orange-hackle streamer tied either "inboard" or "outboard" style with an orange deer hair or trimmed hackle head. PAT FORD PHOTO

was an actual image. There's a point, however, where both of a shark's eyes can focus simultaneously on whatever's in front of it. Call it the "sweet spot." That's where you want your fly to be suspended as the shark makes its move. When it's there, stop stripping!

Another made-to-order situation takes place on the flats. Be it the Keys, the Bahamas, or southwest Florida, sharks are a constant companion on most inshore banks and shallows. They even enter the Intracoastal—especially through Palm Beach, Jupiter, and St. Lucie inlets. The sight of a cruising lemon or bull shark raises few eyebrows in the Lake Worth or Indian River Lagoon. So, will these fish—some weighing upwards of 100 pounds—hit a well-placed fly? I'd say, "Absolutely!"

Sharks have a reputation for taking on all comers, but for fly fishers the major options are large saltwater poppers. The problem with poppers, when you fish from the beach, is that waves pull on the fly line while burying the lure—unless you're able to cast well beyond the shore break. With fly gear, that's quite a challenge—yet still no reason not to put a few in your beach kit. Plus, nothing works better when it comes to bringing up big jack crevalles or large beachcombing bluefish.

Willing sentinels, pelicans perched on weathered pilings guard a silent shell flat. Note the funnel cloud as it licks the far shoreline. PAT FORD PHOTO

Saltwater Bays and Flats

Extending outward from southeast Florida's overstuffed mainland lies an expanse of shallows. These shallows, or flats as we call them, are normally fished by anglers in skiffs. However, walk-in anglers can still gain access—at least, those who have local knowledge. Of the numerous species that inhabit these clear ocean warrens, none draw more attention than the bonefish, permit, and tarpon. Spotted seatrout, snook, and redfish rank right behind them—but that's closer to shore on mangrove-lined, tannic-stained mud banks or in potholes.

All of the above-mentioned species feed heavily on crustaceans (mostly shrimp and crabs). None—with the possible exception of a permit—will ever

Low tide on a marl flat. Mangroves are machines that build islands, create new shorelines, and feed gamefish. PAT FORD PHOTO

Jody Moore's crab flies. The use of crab imitations when targeting permit is a standard practice. JODY MOORE PHOTO

turn down a wounded baitfish. Remember Gartside's Gurgler? Or the many other saltwater "minnows"? Between a crab (or a shrimp) and a baitfish, you've covered the bases.

Carl Ball's Bone Stalker

Captain Carl Ball, of Fort Lauderdale, brings a lifetime of knowledge to Biscayne Bay. That's where the flats stretch from Miami, past Sands Cut and the "Feather Beds," and all the way south to Key Largo. It's in this network of shallows and sea grass–lined channels that Carl pursues bonefish—once considered impossible on fly gear—along with permit and tarpon.

In 1947 angler and outdoor writer Joe Brooks proved that bonefish could be deliberately targeted with flies. Captain Jimmie Albright, of Islamorada, pulled the scales (so to speak) from Joe's eyes when he led Joe to two in one day on fly gear. Since then, a veritable army of anglers has been pursuing these sylph-like gamefish in the shallows of practically every warm ocean. The Bahamas, the Keys, and Biscayne Bay are just a few examples.

Back in the days before the proliferation of all these fancy materials, we'd wade-fish for "tailers" with basic, easy-to-tie patterns. Most were simple, inverted wet flies—featuring little or no tail, chenille bodies, and sparse bucktail wings surrounded by a pair of grizzly hackle tips. At the time, that was all we needed. Then the fishing got tougher.

For Carl, failure isn't an option; that's how he makes his living. Since bonefish stocks aren't near what they used to be, a premium has been put on presentation, as well as on the right imitation. Carl's an accomplished guide and tier, so the burden of proof rests on his anglers. Carl's go-to pattern—the one he reaches for whenever he's guiding—is one he's just started calling Ball's Bone Stalker. Before, it was simply his "bonefish fly." Like he told me, "Eventually, I had to name it *something*."

The Bone Stalker combines a striped Craft Fur (doll hair) wing with plastic bead-chain eyes tied in at the hook bend; a short, brightly colored synthetic tail; a wrapped Puglisi Brush body; and—just behind the hook eye—a set of weighted dumbbell eyes. Carl says he's used it to catch all manner of flats fish, including the "biggies" I mentioned, but, he adds, "Bonefish just can't resist it."

As far as action, Carl (or, usually, his client) casts the fly 5 feet ahead of a cruising bonefish and lets it fall to the bottom. He uses a quick 1-foot strip before stopping to let the fly drop again. He then repeats the process until he comes tight to the fish. In his words: "When you see the bonefish rush the fly and then stop, that's when it eats it. If it did, you'll come tight on the next sharp strip—and in the process, set the hook."

Captain Carl Ball releases a bonefish. CARL BALL PHOTO

Bone Stalker

- **Hook:** #2 Gamakatsu SL11-3H
- **Thread:** Chartreuse Danville's flat waxed nylon
- **Tag:** Orange yarn
- **Eyes:** Black bead chain
- **Tail:** Tan Craft Fur, barred with permanent marker
- **Head:** Medium dumbbell eyes
- **Body:** Sand 1-inch EP Tarantula Hairy Legs Brush
- **Weed guard (optional):** 20-pound Mason hard mono moustache

Tying Tips

1

Tie in the orange yarn tag at the hook bend. Next, secure the black plastic bead chain on top of the yarn.

2

Tie in the Craft Fur ahead of, and on top of, the bead chain.

Wrap the thread all the way forward and tie in the dumbbell.

Wrap the thread all the way back down to the bead chain and tie in the Tarantula Brush.

Reverse direction and wrap the tying thread back to the dumbbell. Wrap the Brush around the shank toward the dumbbell while pulling the fibers toward the hook bend. Tie off the Brush at the dumbbell. If you're adding a weed guard, tie it between the dumbbell and the eye of the hook. After cementing the thread, use the points of your scissors to fluff out the Tarantula Brush body.

Andy Novak's Permit Strategy

Fort Lauderdale tackle shop owner Andy Novak fishes for permit over wrecks in the Gulf of Mexico—where the schools (they're huge) occasionally pop up on the surface. When the sun hits the schools just right . . . Well, we call it "mooning." "Some days, they'll hit," Andy tells me. "Others, they won't." But his surefire solution—when it comes down to the latter—is to toss them a heavily weighted crab on a sinking line and, in his words, "allow it to sink for as much as a minute before beginning a fast-strip retrieve." Sound unconventional? Apparently, the permit don't think so, as evinced by both his and his customers' catches. ■

Andy Novak's quick-sink crab pattern. Del Brown's immortal Merkin started the rush to round, flattened, rug wool bodies. While crab patterns are legion, most exhibit basic similarities: the rug wool body, split hackle "paddles," rubber legs, and dumbbell eyes.

Jon Cave's Wobbler

My late friend and mentor, Mr. Dick Kirkpatrick, who was also the founding editor of *National Wildlife* and a former editor of *Rudder* magazine, was intrigued by the concept of fly-rod lures. I recall us fishing for roadside tarpon and him jumping the one fish of the day on his version of a "spoon fly"—one that he'd fashioned from a strip of Venetian blind.

Jon Cave's version of a spoon fly is extremely effective and a lot more polished than the ones I first fished with Kirkpatrick. What this pattern consists of is a flattened Mylar braid body that's been reinforced with epoxy and fitted with a rabbit skin tail (the latter acts as a drogue or rudder) and a wire moustache weed guard. If you follow Jon's instructions on applying just enough epoxy, you'll end up with a lightweight lure—one that's easy to cast on an 8- or 9-weight outfit. Get one in front of a "tailer" or "cruiser," and I'll bet he'll scarf it.

Jon Cave, inventor of the Wobbler, gets ready to release a red. PAUL CAVE PHOTO

Cave's Wobbler

- **Hook:** #2 Mustad 34011
- **Thread:** 3/0 red Flymaster Plus
- **Body:** Gold, silver, or copper Mylar tubing, approximately 1/2 inch thick
- **Weight:** .015 lead wire
- **Adhesive:** 5-minute epoxy
- **Tail:** Short tapered rabbit strip
- **Weed guard:** Light wire moustache

Tying Tips

1. Grip the hook in pliers and bend the shank forward, in order to create a "cupped" effect. Tie in the tying thread just behind the hook eye, where you'll add five turns of lead wire and cover the wire with thread wraps.
2. Wrap the tying thread back to the exaggerated hook bend.
3. Cut a short piece of Mylar tubing that's slightly longer than the hook. Pull out the stuffing and flatten the tubing (plain ol' ironing may help here).
4. Slide the tubing onto the hook shank and tie off at the bend.
5. Add a short length of tapered rabbit strip at the bend and tie off.
6. Gather the loose ends of Mylar and tie off where you just tied in the rabbit. Trim off the excess. Half-hitch and whip-finish your thread before cutting it, and then reattach the thread at the hook eye.

Jon Cave's innovative Wobbler combines the advantages of both spoon and fly. A "spoon fly" it is, though, with all the affectations (minus the weight) of that redfish staple: the gold wobbling casting spoon.

7. While shaping the tube with your fingers, pull any excess forward before trimming and tying off with your thread at the hook eye.
8. Mix up some two-part 5-minute epoxy, and coat both sides of the Mylar. Allow it to dry while the fly's tilted backward (this keeps most of the weight near the hook bend). Add a second coat later, preferably after a day's worth of drying.
9. You can color the body with a permanent marker, or add a decal eye like I did.

The Tasty Toad

Tarpon aficionado Gary Merriman adapted the Toad from a Del Brown permit fly. Like most of its kind, Del's fly was weighted, so it dove between strips like a crab. But Merriman wanted something that swam straight like a baitfish: something neutrally buoyant that stayed near the surface. He eventually combined a rabbit strip tail with a "pusher" head (sound familiar?), like Del Brown's Merkin—except that the Toad was designed to avoid up-and-down movement. Later, some tiers replaced the rabbit with marabou plume feathers.

Tasty Toad

- **Hook:** Size 2 Gamakatsu SL 12
- **Thread:** Chartreuse 3/0 Monocord
- **Tail:** Chartreuse marabou
- **Body:** Chartreuse poly yarn, tied on Merkin-style, flat in bunches
- **Eyes:** Lead dumbbell, small
- **Weed guard:** Mono moustache

No one can speak to the Toad's effectiveness better than competitive angler Andy Mill. "That's right on the money," said the perennial winner of Keys competitions. "For more than a

Andy Mill, tier and fisher of Toads. He calls this fly a "game changer." Marabou always scores points with tarpon, whether fish that are working the mangroves that abut clear ocean flats or those feeding along muddy back-bay shorelines. ANDY MILL PHOTO

You don't have to be in a flats skiff in order to fish for tarpon. The Toad clone shown in the photo was left in my car by Diana Rudolph when we fished the Tamiami Trail together.

In the mud. Tiny baitfish imitations and bugs that move water (see the salt marsh chapter) both have proven effective in these situations. PAT FORD PHOTO

decade, the Toad was *the* go-to pattern. Over the last twenty years, since 2000, I know of no other tarpon fly that has opened more tarpon faces than this little green machine."

"I don't know exactly why, but my intuition tells me it's how the marabou fibers undulate, even when the angler instills no movement," he added. "Yes, even when lying suspended in the water column, the marabou fibers move and breathe. This pattern has a lifelike presence that practically demands the fish to eat it."

As far as any guesses as to what it represents?

"It doesn't look like anything I've ever seen in the water," Andy admitted. "The chartreuse color must have something to do with it. I'm not sure how much, but I *do* know I get more bites with this color."

Any wild suppositions about why flats tarpon like it?

"It's long and somewhat skinny . . . ballyhoo, pipe fish—I'm not sure—but what I do know is this fly is a powerful tarpon bug!"

Has he any tips on how to fish it?

"I can strip the Toad, slide it, bump it, or even let it hang inert in the water, and the 'poon will eat it. I promise, it was a game changer for many years, and it still has a huge presence in my fly box. Just make sure you don't yank it out of the tarpon's mouth when one explodes on it!"

Old-style "Tarpon Rabbit." These flies, which are crude by modern standards (with their thick tails and heavy flat-forged hooks), were the hot ticket in Islamorada.

American and Hickory Shad

You're walking a sod bank along the St. Johns River, slightly north of Cocoa Beach and south of Lake Harney. Behind you, the floodplain stretches between two distant tree lines. The air reeks of decaying vegetation and the stench of moldering steer dung. The Upper St. Johns virtually oozes through pastures and marshes—dispersing into rivulets that bleed through tussocks before reforming into channels. You sense something primal. Is it the water, or what's moving beneath it? One thing for sure: The St. Johns knows how to hide its secrets—beneath the river's surface, an unseen migration.

The current here runs tannic and torpid, but sometimes it quickens—like where it runs against a sod bank or exits a marsh, or when the wind's pushing behind it. In the past, the St. Johns—which passes just 30 miles west of the Indian River Lagoon—was supposedly part of this ancient fissure that separates the mainland from a series of barrier islands. This detail helps explain an interesting dichotomy: The St. Johns hosts not only freshwater species, such as bass and panfish, but also an intriguing array of saltwater interlopers—including mullet, needlefish, stingrays, and, reportedly, redfish, along with both American and hickory shad, which return to the river to spawn.

Shad require current for their nuptials, and the St. Johns has it—making it America's southernmost river to host a run. The system includes several lakes and innumerable sloughs, so every so often—like when more rain falls downstream than up—the current reverses. Meanwhile, a gentle gradient (approximately 1 inch per mile) helps the current flow from its origins south

Captain Dave Hunt—who's also a Florida Master Naturalist—holds up an American shad taken from the St. Johns River. Shad make an annual spawning run up most East Coast rivers between the St. Johns and Nova Scotia—and now they've been transplanted to the Pacific. Some fish survive to spawn on more than one occasion. Typically, I pursue these fish from the bank, after we find them by boat.

What price peace and quiet? Mike Conner winces as a giant airboat filled with sightseers ruptures the silence.

of Melbourne and Lake Poinsett north to its junction with the Atlantic Ocean, over 300 miles downstream near the Jacksonville metropolis.

As far as the fish themselves? Shad are members of genus *Alosa*, which is closely related to the true herrings, *Brevoortia*. *Alosae* of one variety or another inhabit both sides of the North Atlantic. There's also a shad run (a different species) in the northern Gulf of Mexico, as well as one in the eastern Pacific—in coastal rivers from southern California to the Gulf of Alaska. You can thank auspicious stockings for the latter. Scientists have ascertained that the adults remain in deep offshore waters until they're ready to spawn, at which time they then head for their natal streams in a migration that mimics that of the salmon.

Unlike salmon, however, shad aren't all that specific—meaning they don't always return to their natal rivers. Research suggests that fish from the St. Johns and other southern streams may come from a different genetic stock than those from rivers farther north. Around here, a 4-pounder earns you bragging rights, whereas the Connecticut River once produced an 11¼-pounder. I remember reading about a 13-pounder that was supposedly caught somewhere "up north." Yet I say, if you're interested in old wives' tales, consider the misconception that American shad don't feed after entering fresh water.

Fellow angler Phil Woodham and I have watched them do it for years. Try shaking a few minnows from the next shad you bring to net, or if you keep one for the table, examine it to see what it's been eating. The partially digested remains of tiny baitfish attest to what anglers routinely witness (either knowingly or not) and confuse with "washing": a familiar behavior among shad-fishing circles. It's not uncommon to see dozens of shad feeding on top in the same general area, but don't confuse feeding with washing, a part of their spawning ritual. Scientists may dispute this, yet who can argue with a "bird in the hand"?

Think for a moment: This isn't front-page news. Anglers have been catching shad on flies (that must represent something edible) since the 1930s. That's when pioneers like Tom Loving and Joe Brooks, both of Baltimore, Maryland, cut their teeth (and hands) on the shad of the Chesapeake Bay region. Meanwhile, the credit for popularizing the St. Johns fishery goes to the late Charles Waterman and, to a lesser degree, a fellow named Cather, who manufactured a small trolling spoon of the same name that he used for the purpose. Both men were catching shad on fly tackle by the early 1960s—Cather by trolling from Lemon Bluff to Marina Isle, and Waterman by casting from a skiff in the same general area. That was the golden age of St. Johns shad fishing.

Scientifically speaking, shad are "broadcast spawners" that gather along outside river bends or wherever there's sufficient current to scour the bottom to a depth of 5 or 6 feet. That's also where you'll see fish washing: those violent surface paroxysms that resemble a much-larger salt predator surface-feeding. We locate fish that way, while keeping in mind that washing becomes more prevalent late in the day, as well as later in the season. Shad eggs hatch in the water column, rather than sinking to the bottom.

The Little Richard. When conditions are right, shad explode on this skating pattern. It's nothing but a hot pink spun deer hair "cigar" that I tie with a short, salmon-colored marabou tail on a size 12 4X long-shank hook. There is no hackle or flash.

Traditional shad fishing *can* be fun, but it's still only dredging. Let's be clear on this: Dredging is no longer the *only* means to that end. To our enduring delight, Phil Woodham and I worked out a technique by which shad can be taken on top—with a skating fly. We developed a pattern—the Little Richard—that works like a charm. So what does it represent? Well, we think a chimaera that's part crustacean, part baitfish. How did we come to this split decision?

If you haven't heard, there is (or was) a viable shrimp fishery in the St. Johns below Palatka, and you'll find small baitfish throughout the river. Just watch the marsh terns between wind gusts, or look in the lee of an anchored boat. Shad, unlike salmon, aren't a threat to their offspring, which is why (we think) they fuel their migrations by taking in sustenance. That's how Woodham and I reached this conclusion.

Imagine a glassy run and a tuft of pink deer hair alighting in the afternoon sunlight. It pauses momentarily before starting a cross-stream swing. So far, this differs little from traditional shad fishing, except this time you're using a floating line—instead of a full sink or sink tip—and a longer leader. The fly, which you dressed, is scribbling a wake in the surface film when a boil erupts, and then another, until a 3-pound "roe" shad takes to the air with your fly in her mouth.

Your fly line snaps tight as the fish darts upstream. There's no hesitation, no throbbing indecision. Unlike shad hooked on subsurface patterns, those that hit on top tend to remain there. What follows is a struggle of give and take, but eventually you slide your quarry onto a sloping beach or net it. And there in its mouth is that sliver of pink.

It's all pretty basic: American shad are a schooling species that become seasonally abundant during well-defined "runs." Here in the St. Johns, that season can start as early as Christmas and extend into May (or, on occasion, even longer). I've read that shad in the Delaware River spend all summer in its upper reaches before returning to the sea. That translates to additional spawning potential, while the St. Johns fish supposedly spawn but once before dying. It's ironic—although I'm sure there's a good explanation—but I have yet to see a dead or dying shad (other than ones injured by anglers).

Due to their culinary value, shad also attract commercial interest—the kiss of death for a species that has been in decline. While netters take their share, to a lesser extent so do anglers. For whatever reason, this once-prolific resource has dwindled to the point where the State of Florida imposes a limit of 10 shad per day per person. Since we're talking about a fish that, technically, is a saltwater species that enters freshwater rivers to spawn, the state requires shad fishermen to possess both freshwater and saltwater licenses.

Speaking of resources, while some anglers consider shad roe a delicacy, others disdain any contact with these "halitosis herrings" and release them unharmed. Which brings up a point: It seems antithetical that anything as mundane as a herring could possess much awareness (and therefore deserve a little respect), yet shad are surprisingly high-strung. Accordingly, freshly released fish sometimes attempt to beach themselves or jump back in the boat. If there's a point to this, it's that these fish might not be the mindless rabble we always thought them to be, which is where the skating fly part comes in.

Now here's the subtext: Who can overlook the absurdity of a saltwater fish that rises from the depths of the Sargasso Sea and swims hundreds of miles just to spawn alongside a Central Florida cow pasture? Or the challenge of bringing these enigmas to hand with a tuft of deer hair? Kinda makes you wonder. Like Charley Waterman used to say: "That's what I like about you, Steve. You're always thinkin'."

My answer? "You bet I am."

SHAD FLIES

Typical shad flies are lightly weighted sunken patterns with a few turns of hackle and bead-chain or dumbbell eyes, tied on the gape side of a size 6 Eagle Claw 2X-strong Sproat or Mustad 3908C hook. Of all the classic wet-fly patterns that have emerged over the decades, the ones I prefer over all the others are those I came up with myself. All are color variations of a basic theme. Each one's effectiveness seems to ebb and flood according to light conditions—it's no doubt a matter of visibility.

The Standard

- **Hook:** #6 Eagle Claw 2X-strong Sproat or Mustad 3908C
- **Thread:** Hot orange 8/0
- **Tail:** Tuft of hot orange yarn surrounded by several pearl Krystal Flash fibers
- **Body:** Silver Mylar
- **Hackle:** Several turns of webby white saddle, tied to face backwards
- **Eyes:** Bead chain
- **Note:** The Krypton's Revenge is my go-to pattern for overcast days. Meanwhile, a black variation that I call the Night Stalker performs well under low-light conditions.

The Standard is a good all-around choice, regardless of conditions. It excels, however, on sunny, bluebird days.

Krypton's Revenge

- **Hook:** #6 Eagle Claw 2X-strong Sproat or Mustad 3908C
- **Thread:** Chartreuse 8/0
- **Tail:** Tuft of chartreuse Steelhead Yarn
- **Body:** Gold Mylar
- **Hackle:** Webby chartreuse saddle, a few turns tied down to face backward
- **Eyes:** Bead chain, tied on the gape side

Krypton's Revenge, the author's choice for overcast days.

The Night Stalker

- **Hook:** #6 Eagle Claw 2X-strong Sproat or Mustad 3908C
- **Thread:** Black 8/0
- **Tail:** Tuft of black yarn surrounded by a few fibers of pearl Krystal Flash
- **Body:** Gold Mylar
- **Hackle:** A few turns of webby black saddle tied down to face backwards

The Night Stalker excels late in the day or in stormy conditions.

Index

Note: Locations and waters are in Florida unless otherwise designated.